# UNWAVERING SUCCESS

## with **ERIC STILES**

ALSO FEATURING
OTHER TOP AUTHORS

© 2021 Success Publishing

Success Publishing, LLC
P.O. Box 703536
Dallas, Texas 75370 USA

questions@mattmorris.com

All rights reserved. No part of this book may be reproduced, stored in a retrieval system, or transmitted in any form or by any means - electronic or mechanical, photocopy, recording, or any other - except for brief quotations in printed reviews, without the prior permission of the publisher. Although the author(s) and publisher have made every effort to ensure the accuracy and completeness of information contained in this book, we assume no responsibility for errors, inaccuracies, omissions, or any inconsistency herein.

"Through years of professional workforce experience, Eric has a formula for making everyone with whom he surrounds himself a better leader. Focused and driven, he is constantly developing those around him to succeed. A brilliant mind with a passion for sharing leadership principles and producing achievers."

—Charles Copeland

First Sergeant US Army (Retired), Former CIA Contractor

"Eric leads by example in every aspect. As an Engineering Officer aboard our prototype fast ferry in Brazil for five years, he not only exceeded expectations, he demonstrated leadership that offered the lessons of a true maritime professional who has been there. He's taught countless others through talent and example."

—R.T. Douville

Commander, USCG (Retired),

Industrial Compliance Expert, Trico International

"Eric was my first-line supervisor as a young soldier. For the rest of my career, until my retirement as Lieutenant Colonel, his positive influence in my early years was my benchmark to evaluate NCOs. He worked hard, played hard, and mentored his troops to be the best they could be."

—Richard J. Meace

LTC, LG, US Army (Retired), Operations Expert

"Eric Stiles took charge of keeping a vessel operating in a foreign country, and if it was not for his leadership in getting all crew members working together and pulling in the same direction, this operation would have been shut down and cost the company a lot of money. Eric leads by example. He not only talks the talk but also walks the walk. Eric takes care of his teammates. As a Maritime Master, I would love to have Eric working with me on any type of project."

—George E. Drury Jr.

US Merchant Marine Master Mariner, Vessel Master

*"In life, one's attitude can determine an individual's trajectory through life. Working with Eric, I have witnessed how someone's attitude can turn around a floundering team. Eric's leadership and "get it done" attitude turned a substandard operating team into an elite group of high-performing team members. His leadership abilities with clearly defined expectations set the standard while guiding his subordinates to success. True leadership is neither the position you hold nor the office you occupy, it is the results that you can yield while developing those around you, helping them to excel and reach their potential."*

—Nick Mayon
HSE Manager, All Coast, LLC, Industrial Operations Expert

*"I have known Eric since 1981. He has proven himself to be an excellent example of what a leader should be, know and do. Eric has phenomenal intelligence and is a go-getter! He is one of the best soldiers, teachers, and technicians that I ever have seen! Eric was always picked for new equipment that came into the field. He is the BEST!"*

—Russell Trogdon
CW4 US Army (Retired),
Former Chief of US Army Marine Trades School

# Table of Contents

1. Comradery Over Intimidation:
   Building Teams Because Things Can Always Be Worse . . . . . . . . 9
   *By Eric Stiles*

2. From Bound To Boundless . . . . . . . . . . . . 17
   *By Matt Morris*

3. Scared Shitless . . . . . . . . . . . . . . . . . 25
   *By Steve Moreland*

4. Pause, Think And Stay Authentic . . . . . . . . . . . . . . . . 33
   *By Amy Ruzicka*

5. There's No Such Thing As Failure . . . . . . . . . . . . . . . . 39
   *By Anthony Pierre*

6. Metamorphosis Is My Story Of Becoming . . . . . . . . . . . 45
   *By B. Heather Pinard*

7. Don't Find An Excuse, Find A Way . . . . . . . . . . . . . 53
   *By Bobbie Hall*

8. What Is Your True Purpose? . . . . . . . . . . . . . . . . . . . 59
   *By David Minshall*

9. Just Keep Pushing . . . . . . . . . 67
   *By Denver Duncan*

10. No U-Turns, Gps, And Foot Checks . . . . . . . . . . . . . . . 73
    *By Donna Shupe*

11. Why I Did Not Give Up When It Was
    The Easiest Thing To Do . . . . . . . . . . . . . . . . . . . 79
    *By Douglas Chee*

12. New Beginnings . . . . . . . . . . . . . . . . . . . . . 87
    By Elizabeth McCoon

13. Pain As A Catalyst . . . . . . . . . . . . . . . . . . . 93
    By Eric Ranks

14. Walking Down The Road With A Gas Can . . . . . . . . . 101
    By Greg Theobald

15. Your New Diagnosis: Pain-Free . . . . . . . . . . . . . 107
    By Guillermo De Novi

16. What Now? . . . . . . . . . . . . . . . . . . . . . . . 115
    By Jacob Long

17. Deep-Rooted Success From Self-Empowerment . . . . . . . 121
    By Jannette Tomamao

18. Adversity . . . . . . . . . . . . . . . . . . . . . . . 129
    By John Kelly

19. The Hero's Journey . . . . . . . . . . . . . . . . . . 135
    By John Kennedy

20. Solving The Rubik's Cube Of Network Marketing . . . . . 143
    By Karyn Mahoney

21. The Deeper Why . . . . . . . . . . . . . . . . . . . . 151
    By Leah Clout

22. Use The Gifts You've Received In Life! . . . . . . . . 157
    By Leif Näsberg

23. Box? What Box? . . . . . . . . . . . . . . . . . . . . 165
    By Lori Ryan

24. Born For Greatness . . . . . . . . . . . . . . . . . . 171
    By Martine Viney

25. Searching For The Smartest Way To Make A Good Life . . . . . . . 177
    By Morten Andersen

26. Thrive In Adversity . . . . . . . . . . . . . . . . . . . . . . . 185
    By Patrice Maurer

27. Higher Way Of Life . . . . . . . . . . . . . . . . . . . . . . . 193
    By Patty Carson

28. From Fear To Faithfulness . . . . . . . . . . . . . . . . . . . . 199
    By Philip Booth

29. Growing A Side Business Into A Full-Time Income . . . . . . . . 207
    By Phillipa Nanyondo Wavamunno Byamah

30. Finish What You Start . . . . . . . . . . . . . . . . . . . . . . 215
    By Regina Nunnally

31. Help Wanted: Hire Yourself . . . . . . . . . . . . . . . . . . . 221
    By Reginald Dockery

32. Focus Is The Catalyst . . . . . . . . . . . . . . . . . . . . . . 231
    By Robert Peizer

33. The Power Of Being Wrapped In Love . . . . . . . . . . . . . . 239
    By Tansy Serediak

34. Hanging On Faith . . . . . . . . . . . . . . . . . . . . . . . . 245
    By Venice Hughes

CHAPTER 1

# Comradery Over Intimidation: Building Teams Because Things Can Always Be Worse

*By Eric Stiles*

Raised on a farm in western Pennsylvania, I grew up going full throttle at all times, regularly experiencing extreme events. The counseling I received consistently amounted to: 'It can always be worse.' And usually, it was.

The first incident I recall was before we moved to our farm. We lived in Akron, Ohio, where my mother and I were trapped in the race riots. We were alone in our car; I was just a little seven-year-old. The terrorists had stopped traffic and were flipping over vehicles and tossing firebombs. My mother told me, "Get Daddy's pistol out of the glove compartment." I did and handed it to her as a mob approached us, breaking car windows and dragging people out of their cars.

She fired several warning shots and slowed the threat. "See if there are any more bullets," she calmly told me. There were two more magazines, so I gave them to her. In a short time, some Army jeeps pulled up and dispersed the mob with some small arms fire and a few .30 caliber machine-gun bursts.

The troops in jeeps spoke to my mother a bit and advised her which direction to escape. She was twenty-eight or so, blonde, with a good figure. So those guys were very helpful.

I'll never forget one of the jeep drivers with a cigarette dangling from his grinning mouth. "Put that gun away now, sonny. You'll get your chance. It can always be worse!" he said with a wink.

As we neared home, I asked my mother, "Can I be an Army man when I grow up?"

"Sure, you can. Not sure Daddy would approve." During that time, my father served as a Marine in Vietnam. As soon as my father returned a few months later, we moved to our farm in the mountains of western Pennsylvania.

We carved out a functional business from the steep, wet, and rocky terrain. The winters were brutal, leaving us snowbound and without electricity for long periods. 'It can always be worse,' I remember wondering for the first time. Okay, this is our attitude, but what is the solution?

In 1972, Hurricane Agnes hit the area hard, pretty much destroying everything we had built so far. "It can always be worse," my father quipped as we removed the rotting corpses of our drowned livestock from the barn wreckage. "Just think, in Cambodia, right now, all this would be dead people. Smells about the same." I remember wondering again about the solution to recover and witnessed that the answer was teamwork. Voluntary teamwork.

In 1973 we enjoyed the Arab Oil Embargo. "It can always be worse," and it was. My mother suffered a stroke that paralyzed her left side. Again, voluntary teamwork and community support made things better. She hasn't had the use of her left arm ever since and suffers a permanent Captain Ahab limp. Talk about a tough lady; she'll tell you that it can always be worse to this day.

The Johnstown flood of 1977 came and went, once more destroying just about everything everyone in the area had built and killing more than eighty people. It can always be worse. I vigorously participated in recovery efforts by building and leading teams. The way we teamed up just made sense (common goals were crystal clear), and I observed how teamwork materializes. Back then, in that area, emergency personnel were volunteers. Again, voluntary teamwork and community support made things better.

During my mid to late teens, I put together teams for projects such as building barns, silos, fencing, harvesting, storing crops, and overhauling machinery. I quickly realized that when people worked together, they produced more efficiently, enjoyed the teamwork, learned from each other, and formed personal bonds based on group success and actual fun. "It can always be worse" helped when things became difficult.

In 1980, many farmers lost everything due to two years of bad weather and a faltering economy. Our farm was one of them. The Selective Service was reinstated, and it looked like we were going to war with Iran. Most of my friends were in their early thirties, served in Vietnam. They all had scars and wounds that were quite bad. To a man, they suggested that guys my age should join the service before getting drafted so we could pick a job that would be less dangerous and provide a trade later on. Because it certainly could always be worse.

I joined the Army because they had the best job selection, and they said I would go to Hawaii for four years. So, I enlisted to be a boat mechanic. Yes, a boat mechanic. In the Army. Army ships remain an unknown asset to this day.

I thought this would teach me super-organized teamwork. Wow. I was in for a surprise.

I found that the leadership and teamwork I initially experienced in the Army were based on threat, coercion, and intimidation. So, I took it. Everyone else did as well because it could be worse.

When I got to my boat mechanic training in Virginia, I found that the others in my group were pretty sharp and friendly fellows who were all already pretty good scientists, electricians, and mechanics. We all had a common goal: complete our school and go to work, all the while demonstrating to our overlords that we could take anything they could dish out. And dish out, they did. It could always be worse.

We had a class leader who wore the red airborne beret, a Vietnam combat patch, and a Combat Infantry Badge. He was very kind to us and showed us how to enjoy working hard. He helped us form into a tight team, and we won all contests and successfully overcame challenges while continuously learning from each other.

I remember feeling that this was the way teamwork should be done. We were so tight that I did some stupid things without giving them a second thought because I had become a super brilliant tech and a physical animal. It could always be worse. So, I made it worse.

We had a classroom instruction about fuel pumps. Fairly simple. But the instructor could barely read. He was pathetic, and everyone was giggling. Eventually, we had to fill out a critique, so I suggested that we no longer be subject to endure illiterate instructors who were unfamiliar with the subject. Things became worse.

Our class received plenty of physical torture with the intent of getting someone to confess. When we got a break, I went to our class leader and told him that I wrote the offending critique. "I know that, Eric. Nobody cares more about getting everything right than you. Because to you, it's instinctive to correct problems before they cause more problems and things get worse, right?"

"But everyone is suffering because of me."

"Shut your mouth and learn your lesson. Nobody will rat you out. That would make our team weaker. Learn your lesson," said our class leader.

I'm sure the cadre figured out that I was the one, but nobody ratted, and eventually, they got tired of torturing us because we took it all with a smile. It could always be worse.

I learned that lesson so hard and well that I did another stupid thing as my pendulum swung the other way. The class leader recommended to the commander that I should attend USMAPS: a prep school with the opportunity to attend West Point. I turned it down because I wanted to be with my team. Pretty dumb.

Then our class leader got killed in a motorcycle wreck. It could always be worse.

My first assignment was as an oiler on the Army's biggest ship in Hawaii. My sergeants were angry all the time and seemed to really hate all new guys. I later found that they were very protective of their positions because they were not very competent at engine room operations. The officers never showed them anything. It could always be worse.

I was cleaning engine parts with a fellow young soldier one day while two sergeants watched. There were some parts that we couldn't quite disassemble right away, and the sergeants laughed at us, called us names, and threatened us.

One of them said, "So you're so stupid that you can't figure that out?"

I looked him square in the eye, fully prepared to take my ass-kicking, punishment, extra duty, whatever. I said, "Yeah, I am. Now, why don't you do your job and show me how?"

Those guys looked at each other, and they never stopped sharing everything they knew with everyone they met. They both became Sergeant Majors, and we are all good friends to this day.

I worked hard and learned harder. I was promoted quickly, sent to many challenging schools, and instructed many of them.

I learned some teambuilding lessons the hard way. That was always because I didn't consult more experienced people first.

We grew the Army's lifelong leadership development program continuously, always working closely with civilian psychology experts. We did so well that we got our NCO Academies accredited through universities.

It could always be worse. The Army had a huge purge in the late 1990s. I was suddenly a civilian. My job paid very well, and the engineering work was familiar. But I noticed that there were no decent teams, and "do what I say, or you're fired" was normal as turnover was high. Nobody was happy or did anything to prevent things from getting worse.

Right away, I was selected to run an expensive, revolutionary, new vessel-type project. I told them something like that would require a team (which nobody in the organization had done)—not a team that operated separately from the rest of the company, but one that would offer participation and opportunity for everyone. They laughed and mentioned that most of the employees were too stupid to understand things like that. That was the heart of their "It could be worse" scenario.

And worse it became. The company went public, and people at and near the top became millionaires. They paid just enough for the ship's crews to keep people from quitting. As people did quit, nobody took their place. Everything was overbudget, and everyone who could steal, embezzle, and pad their expense account did it as hard as they could. No teamwork at all. They were bankrupt within five years.

The greatest team that I ever worked with was on an offshore crane barge with a 275-member crew. We had to make sweeping changes, so we decided to have the entire crew define their specific jobs and procedures in writing. These procedures were converted into safety briefings and permits. This, combined with a generous monthly safety bonus for all, resulted in excellent, safe, and efficient work. The deal was that if there was a single lost-time incident or downtime, absolutely no one would receive their bonus. The people had to watch each other's backs, and everyone is great friends to this day. Suddenly, unreasonable federal regulations crushed this company. It can always be worse.

I worked in several other teams—the best and the worst. The worst was always infected with a toxic, intimidating dictatorship. The best relied upon participative teamwork.

Some of the key points I've come to rely upon are as follows:

1. It can always be worse. We can't predict what's next, but we can always strive to prepare.

2. Teamwork is the answer to most problems. No one can know everything.

3. People instinctively want to be part of groups and teams. Team members should be volunteers.

4. Teams must have common goals among all members.

5. Team members need to share knowledge and skills amongst themselves.

6. A team's members and functioning need to be cohesive but should not be exclusive within the organization.

I don't use the terms 'leader' and 'leadership.' 'Activity Coordinator' is more suitable. 'Leader' is more of a title with today's changing language. It implies superiority over the team.

The activity coordinator must have core competencies, provide direction and resources, and stimulate action through comradery. Things could be worse, and we are all in this together.

The entire organization must be one large team with common goals.

Special project teams should be temporary.

Performance bonuses are the best way to get people to join teams and make them thrive.

Those who threaten and intimidate are rarely successful, and nobody wants to be a part of that team.

It's just my experience. There are many excellent former teammates who say I'm a great leader, and they have me teaching leadership in colleges to this day. I just consider myself a solid, reliable teammate. Because things can always be worse.

## BIOGRAPHY

Eric Stiles is a US Merchant Marine Engineering Officer and Leadership Instructor at Marine Training Institutions around the country. With a lifetime of experience in teambuilding and leadership instruction, Eric has become a sought-after authority on the subject. In this work, his personal worldwide experiences are related to how and why teambuilding works. Mr. Stiles is a US Army veteran. He wrote doctrine and taught Leadership at NCO Academies. He has an MSA in Organizational Administration from Central Michigan University. He has an undergraduate degree from Saint Leo University in Liberal Arts, and he graduated summa cum laude while on active duty, attending college at night and teaching during the day. Mr. Stiles led many cutting-edge projects in the Southern Hemisphere offshore industry, building a reputation as 'the guy you want to work with.' He lives with his family in Ocala, Florida, where he runs a business and a charity.

Contact Eric Stiles via https://linktr.ee/enstiles

CHAPTER 2

# From Bound To Boundless

*By Matt Morris*

As a speaker and coach for the past 20 years, I've been blessed to help several thousand people become full-time entrepreneurs with hundreds in the six-figure range and over 50 documented million-dollar earners.

It's also rewarded me with a lifestyle that I never would have imagined as a boy. If you would have told me I'd be a millionaire at twenty-nine, earn eight figures in my thirties and generate several billion in sales, all while adventuring to over 80 countries by my early 40's; I wouldn't have believed you.

I also never imagined I'd be blessed with a career that fills me up with such immense levels of fulfillment and significance, knowing that I've been able to assist so many others in achieving what most would consider "boundless" levels of success.

The question I'm asked all the time is . . . How?

In asking that question, most people are looking for the tactics and strategies. And I'll admit, early in my coaching days, I focused my mentorship almost solely on teaching the how-tos.

Unfortunately, that made me a pretty lousy coach.

I'd give them the tactics that allowed me to become a superstar salesperson, run a multi-million dollar company, or speak powerfully from stage.

My students would apply the how-tos and come back frustrated with mediocre improvements at best.

What I failed to realize in my early coaching days is a quote from the late Brian Klemmer that says, "If how-tos were enough, we'd all be rich, skinny, and happy."

As we explore the secrets to experiencing boundless levels of success, we must first examine what keeps us bound to our current situation.

Hint: It's NOT a lack of tactics and strategies.

With a quick google search, you can find hundreds of YouTube videos and blog posts that will teach you the strategies to having six-pack abs. The reason most don't have that six-pack isn't that they don't know the how-tos.

When it comes to making your goals a reality, whether that be to have a sexy body, to become a top sales leader in your company, to start your own business, or any other worthwhile dream, the ONLY thing holding you back from achieving that goal is your mental programming.

The challenge most face in achieving a grand visionary future for themselves is the fact that it runs so completely contrary to their current vision, or identity, that's running them now.

Your current identity is made up of the beliefs you currently hold to be true about yourself. It's essentially how you genuinely see yourself.

Your personal identity subconsciously influences every decision and action you make (or don't make), thus influencing the level of success you're able to achieve.

If your personal identity is that of someone who is out of shape or overweight, you may go on streaks where you eat right and exercise vigorously, but you tend to always shift right back into your old ways. Irresistible cravings, lethargy, sleeping in, etc., are somehow always overpowering your desire to be fit.

Why is that the case?

You'll want to write this down.

## The Law of Commitment and Consistency

*The law of commitment and consistency says that we will remain committed to remaining consistent with who we genuinely believe we are.*

That being true, we must understand that in order to change our results, we have to change the beliefs we have about ourselves.

Let's take a deep dive into beliefs.

Take a look at the middle three letters of the word "beliefs," and what word do you see?

LIE

Consider for a moment that the story (the beliefs) you've been telling yourself about who you are as a person are simply lies you've made up.

Stories you may have accepted as "fact" like you're:

- Shy
- Self-conscious
- Lack self-confidence
- Not a morning person
- Afraid of public speaking
- Not a good communicator
- Not as smart as the others

Would it be empowering to know that any of the negative beliefs above, along with countless others, are nothing more than lies you created subconsciously through a belief-building process you went through and didn't even know you were going through it?

What makes me so certain these "character traits" are lies? Because I had all of those beliefs about myself that I once accepted as fact.

Today, if you told me I was any of those things, I would laugh in your face because it would be completely absurd in my mind to accept any of those as true.

If you're willing to take a journey with me, I'll show you how I literally rewrote my entire identity from a broke, scarcity-filled, self-conscious young man into a confident and powerful multi-millionaire.

I'm here to tell you that whatever limiting beliefs you've created for yourself are absolute and total crap. I'm proof of it and many of those I've mentored for the past 20 years are proof of it.

I don't know what lies about yourself you've accepted as fact, but I know beyond a shadow of a doubt that, at your core, you are not a bad communicator, you are not unworthy of finding love, you are not a failure, you are not destined to always struggle, or any other negative belief.

Whatever they might be, you have the power to change those disempowering beliefs that serve only to limit the amount of success and personal fulfillment you experience.

If your current beliefs are what determine your success, the big question becomes how do you change your beliefs to create the results you want?

Before we answer that question, you first need to understand what shapes your beliefs in the first place. What has caused you to hold the beliefs that you do? Understanding where they came from will help you change them.

The belief building process you went through to come up with the beliefs you currently hold to be true have been shaped by three main factors:

1. Experiences
2. External programming
3. Internal programming

**Experiences:**

Every experience you've ever been through has been forever deposited and stored somewhere in your subconscious mind.

Maybe you were teased as a kid in school because you stuttered, and now you believe you're a poor communicator. Maybe, you were laughed at in class as a kid for giving the wrong answer, and you took on a belief that you're not as smart as the other kids. Maybe you made a few horrible business choices when you were first starting out, and now you think you're lousy in business.

Whether you've realized it before now or not, those deposits were the first major factor that gave you the foundation of your identity.

Here's the way it works . . .

An event happens and then you make up a story (a belief) about what that event means.

Most of us tend to create a negative meaning based on what we perceive to be a negative experience. We create a victim story – I'm not loved because my parent abused me or left me. I'm a terrible business person because I failed for five years. People are not trustworthy because my business partner stole from me (all personal stories I made up at one point).

Think about some examples from your past. Can you think of some examples of events where you created a negative belief?

***Real power comes from understanding that nothing has meaning until we give it meaning.***

Events are neutral. It's the story we make up from the event that holds all the power. Rather than the victim story you may have been running in your mind, how can you create a new and empowering meaning based on that experience?

Understand – you have the power to choose. Victim or Victor. Which will it be?

**External Programming:**

Whether you want to believe this or not, you've been programmed.

Your parents programmed you as a child to believe certain things about yourself, other people, money, religion, and many other things.

The school system, your friends, the media, television, and other factors have programmed you to believe many of the things you do today.

Some of this programming has likely been healthy and gotten you to where you are and built you into the person you are today. Unfortunately, we also all have some less than empowering beliefs, and associated fears, that we've adopted as well from that external programing.

By the time you were two years old, you heard the word no thousands of times more than you heard the word yes. It's no wonder so many people, when presented with an opportunity to start a business or take on a challenge, are paralyzed with fear and are hesitant to take action.

At some point in your life, you've most likely faced a moment where someone said something negative to you or doubted your ability, without even meaning to. For a lot of people, that first comes from their parents and family members.

The things that people say to you, whether they intentionally mean harm or not, can profoundly shape who you are—*but only if you let it*. You obviously can't go back into the past and change the negative things you've heard, but you can make the decision right now to no longer let those things define you.

You can recognize that what someone says about you has no basis in reality unless you *choose* to believe it. It's a choice. A choice you can start making right now, today, to say **no more**.

**Internal Programming:**

More than your experiences and more than the voices of the people around you, the greatest and most powerful way your beliefs are shaped is from your internal programming. Thankfully, it's also the mechanism you have the most control over.

Every word that comes out of your mouth and every thought that comes out of your mind serves as a programming tool. Those thoughts and words get entered into your subconscious mind and then work to create your habitual routines and mental thought patterns.

Psychologists who study brain science agree that your subconscious mind is infinitely more powerful than your conscious mind. The subconscious is the driving force behind your belief system and your identity.

The subconscious mind has a goal that can serve you negatively or positively. That goal is to keep you in line with your identity. Remember the law of commitment and consistency?

If, based on your regular programming, you tell yourself you're broke, you're tired, and you suck as an entrepreneur, your subconscious mind figures out a way to keep you consistent with that programming.

If, however, you continually tell yourself you're wealthy, you're energized, and you're an amazing entrepreneur, your subconscious mind begins doing everything in its power to create *that* reality.

Here's the best way to understand it.

**Whatever you say about yourself makes it more true.**

If you say, *"I'm an idiot,"* you become more of an idiot. If you say, *"I'm a genius,"* you become more of a genius.

Your consistent programming creates your identity.

Here's the trick; your subconscious mind does not know the difference between the truth and a lie. It simply does its best to carry out exactly what you've programmed it to believe.

So when you say, "I'm sexy, I'm confident, I'm a millionaire," your conscious mind might be telling you you're full of it, but your subconscious mind, which is where the true power lies, will take that as a command and start working out a way for you to be all of those things.

The key to reprogramming your subconscious and change your deep-seeded beliefs is to change your deposits. You do this by constantly filling your subconscious mind with empowering, uplifting, and motivating thoughts and words.

If you continually profess what you don't want, or focus on the things you don't have or aren't, then you actually attract more of that negativity and continue to reinforce more of that personal identity. ***What you focus on expands***.

## BIOGRAPHY

Author of the international bestseller, *The Unemployed Millionaire*, Matt Morris began his career as a serial entrepreneur aged eighteen. Since then, he has generated over $1.5 billion through his sales organizations, with a total of over one million customers worldwide. As a self-made millionaire and one of the top internet and network marketing experts, he's been featured on international radio and television and spoken from platforms to audiences in over twenty-five countries around the world. And now, as the founder of Success Publishing, he co-authors with leading experts from every walk of life.

Contact Matt Morris via http://www.MattMorris.com

CHAPTER 3

# Scared Shitless

*By Steve Moreland*

How do you keep from tossing in the towel at age thirty-five because a twenty-five-year prison sentence for crimes you did not commit is just a bridge too far?

As I read G. K. Chesterton's book *Orthodoxy* one night inside that icy, cement cell, it felt like a ray of hope had pierced the dark maze that often felt like a grave.

"Courage is almost a contradiction in terms. Valor means a strong desire to live, taking the form of a readiness to die. 'He that will lose his life, the same shall save it' is not a piece of mysticism for saints and heroes. It is a piece of everyday advice for sailors and mountaineers. It might be printed in an Alpine guide or a drill book. The paradox is the whole principle of courage, even of quite earthly or quite brutal courage. A man cut off by the sea may save his life if he will risk it on the precipice. He can only get away from death by continually stepping within an inch of it. A soldier surrounded by enemies, if he is to cut his way out, needs to combine a strong desire for living with a strange carelessness about dying. He must not merely cling to life, for then he will be a coward, and will not escape. He must not merely wait for death, for then he will be a suicide, and will not escape. **He must seek his life** *in a spirit of furious indifference to it; he must desire life like water and yet drink death like wine."*

I was trained to believe the test of a man is what it takes to stop him. Grit is what it's called in Texas. It's brutal. And it's not about anything other than performance, because no one cares to hear your weak, sniveling excuses. So, you grow up learning how to numb the pain of the sun burning the back of your neck and from suffocating in the 110-degree, breezeless terrain. You get used to the burnt grass, the scrub pines, the desolate landscapes, and the intolerant demands for excellence from a decorated war hero called Dad.

The first time I came home beat up at age twelve by three fourteen-year-olds, I expected some sympathy. But boy, was I mistaken! I revered his service to our country as a Marine, whose last mission to destroy an embedded bunker on the DMZ in Vietnam in 1968 resulted in half the recon team KIA (killed in action) and the other half WIA (wounded in action). Valor, in the face of overwhelming force, had caused his thousand-yard stare that freaked out most people. But to me, he was Dad.

After explaining how I'd been jumped by three bigger boys, he began demonstrating techniques to snap their necks or break their spines. In utter disbelief, I argued that I could not murder them. And then his emotionless response caused my heart to sink, when he replied, "Okay, then, if you come home beaten up again, I'll beat you worse."

Talk about jumping from the frying pan and into the fire! My heart stopped. I had gone to him for help. But instead, I was sure my days on earth were numbered because I cried to the wrong Marine. And yet, the next time Jeff Hayes came after me, I reacted with a level of force that terrified me. It wasn't pretty. It wasn't Bruce Lee level awesome. It came out of sheer terror. What some call scared shitless! And to my amazement, it worked.

In life, you're first given the test, later the lesson.

Life has rarely made sense to me. You'd think we'd get an instruction manual explaining how to solve life's challenges. Instead, we often get advice from "armchair quarterbacks" who hide from any real risk because they've never learned how to perform the common (duties) under uncommon conditions. They give you tons of "ideas" that are as worthless as those theories blathered by our business professors, who have never spent a single day performing in the real world.

He'd sadly pronounced at an early age that I didn't have a lick of athletic talent, so I was ordered to make first-squad by out-practicing everyone else. I worked extra hard until the coach felt guilty for not letting me play—raw discipline fueled by being scared shitless not to measure up to Dad's expectations.

Years later, I found myself fighting in martial art tournaments for the thrill and outrunning state troopers on my Kawasaki Ninja motorcycle at over 100 MPH to supply that "fix" of scared shitlessness. Later, it was fighting in parking lots against half of the offensive line of some goat-roping town out in the sticks nearby or joy-riding in stolen cars. Recklessness had become my drug of choice.

Then, as fate would have it, I accidentally won academic scholarships and Dad forbade me to enlist in his beloved Marine Corps. His "change of orders" was to get a degree from those professors with little to no experience, and return to the Corps and lead as an officer instead of battle-proven Gunnery Sergeant. So, what did I do but blow up my scholarships with my disrespectful comments to the dean of business, when he refused my challenge to compare his tax return to mine. You see, in 1986, I'd reported over $40,000 from my part-time grass mowing business, when I wasn't working out, playing point guard on the squad, or traveling with the TaeKwonDo team. So, after my BCD (Marine lingo for a "bad conduct discharge") from my scholarships, I sought out a new challenge to redeem myself in the eyes of the Marine I feared I could never equal in acts of valor.

I ran headfirst into corporate America after watching the movie *Wall Street*. Though I outperformed the guys with the degrees (that I secretly envied), my addiction demanded more. So I became a workaholic. And when the pedigreed boys laughed me out of their Monday morning sales meetings for my atypical marketing ideas, I didn't curl up in a fetal position like most folks would. I got angry, crazy-mad with revenge. I showed up earlier, stayed later, worked all weekend. I then added to my regimen the discipline of listening to personal mindset development cassette tapes. One after another, while speeding all over Dallas until that wasn't enough. So I went to sleep with more subliminal tapes playing in the background—scared shitless that my lack of natural talent would prove me unworthy by comparison. I was determined to train my mind to think better, react faster, and perform with less apprehension of risks. To win, or die trying . . . if that's what it took!

And it worked! I'd traded in my dream of becoming a lifer as a gunnery sergeant in the U.S. Marine Corps, like Clint Eastwood's character in *Heartbreak Ridge,* to become Bud Fox in the 1985 film *Wall Street.* I ranked as the top producer in several Fortune 500 companies before I was twenty-five, started my own brokerage agency for a Canadian insurance juggernaut shortly thereafter, and fearlessly catapulted myself into the shark-infested waters of offshore private banking and venture capital investing, all before age thirty. I was prouder of my titles than my eight-figure net worth: director of offshore operations for my mentor's hedge fund based in Turks and Caicos, president of a fifty-eight-office trust and accounting firm based in Utah, and co-principal in a pre-IPO SaaS technology company in California.

And then the phone call came the day after returning home from our international shareholder's event in Vegas. The voice rambled on about the Feds raiding our offices, freezing all our accounts, and the founder being held in his house at gunpoint.

Since I was under the assumption that we'd been attacked without any justification and because I was being groomed to take over the reigns of the company in the next ten years, technically, I was now in command. So, everyone was waiting for my decisions amidst the absolute chaos.

Finally, war had found me. I was going to get my chance to prove my worth. And I performed with ice in my veins.

I defended our operation to prevent further wrongdoing by what I believed to be just another Jeff Hays bully coming to kick my ass. Within twenty-four hours, I had secured our offshore holdings that hadn't been discovered, relocated our command and control to a foreign country, and caused several thousand investors to literally disappear from the open internet and onto an encrypted server based in Ireland. In Dad's lingo, I'd successfully hardened communications, reinforced HQ, and secured our resources.

And boy, did I piss off the wrong gang of bullies!

By July 2002, I was inside a ten-week federal money-laundering and investment fraud trial. The prior fourteen months from federal detention in Seattle was a blur of filing motions against the U.S. attorneys, though I'd never been to law school. And by September, I was taking the stand to fight the senior prosecutor, *mano a mano*. Many of the other co-defendants had lied because they were scared shitless and had taken plea bargains to reduce their prison sentences to under five years. I refused, purely out of principle, even ignoring a direct order from Dad to break our family honor code and take the ten-year plea bargain deal.

> "A man is never more than a man than when he embraces an
> adventure beyond his control, or when he walks into a battle
> he isn't sure of winning."—John Eldridge

In the middle of such extreme risk, there's no such thing as fearlessness: There's feeling the fear and acting the right way regardless. So I learned that real performance is just continuing to engage, even when you're scared shitless. It's finding that space called faith. Not faith in the Creator but faith in your ability to endure levels of agony that would cause the hearts of most to seize up.

In Will Smith's movie *After Earth*, he plays the character of a valiant general attempting to guide his son on a perilous mission. His son had already failed Ranger school, but now their lives depended on him doing the impossible.

"Fear is not real. The only place that fear can exist is in our thoughts of the future. It is a product of our imagination, causing us to fear things that do not at present, and may not, ever exist. That is near insanity. Do not misunderstand me, danger is very real. But fear is a choice."

I lost at trial! Yet I continued my mission, fighting another year from detention, only to secure a seemingly minor win of a 292-month sentence instead of the life sentence in federal prison that the gang of bullies requested from the judge. When I walked onto my first yard in Beaumont, Texas, in October 2003, I was nicknamed "the yacht man" because of my once-upon-a-time wealth. It would eventually become "Sergeant Slaughter."

Amid the daily struggle against life's scum and with zero reinforcements, I secured three consecutive wins in the circuit appellate courts, more than any other white-collar, first-time, non-violent offender in history. But the real trophy was reversing my own case in the United States Supreme Court in 2009. And while fighting these near-impossible obstacles, the mother of my children turned on me during an ugly divorce and attempted to take away my rights as a father and erase me from the lives of my two children. Her father warned her, "Dumb mistake, Steve doesn't surrender!"

For 5,544 days, I marched across hell. The demons walking the halls at night relentlessly whispered that I was a fool, insane, exhibiting conduct unbecoming of a father and husband. And maybe they were right. Perhaps I should have acted like a coward and broken our family's honor code by lying about doing something I did not. Perhaps I should have set the example for my children by giving lip service to my creed but breaking weak when life got ugly. That's what most others would have done . . . and then justified their cowardice with lame excuses.

From experience, not theory, I can tell you there are no perfect solutions to impossible scenarios. So I'll share with you how I reasoned why I was being tortured. I penned an essay in 2007 entitled *A Perfect Imperfection* and published it on my blog from prison. My blog is called

Tsyo Matte, samurai lingo for "Be Strong!" (https://tsuyomatte.wordpress.com/).

> Therefore we must ask ourselves what makes our heroes heroic? Are they perfect? Hardly. What makes a hero so heroic isn't that he's perfect, but that he is imperfect. A hero is a person who overcomes his own limitations, transcends his weaknesses, and stands his ground when most retreat to excuses. He becomes, in effect, a perfect imperfection, just as a perfect storm achieves its terrifying strength through a perfect combination of imperfect—that is to say, disorderly—elements. Valor can only be found in these most imperfect of places, confusing places, that leave behind clues of "how" the few performed, and more importantly, "why." These characteristics conceal themselves; they hide within enigmas and paradoxes—buried inside legends, lore, and myths. And the cardinal paradox cloaking itself within the imperfect chaos of battle is a pure and relentless allegiance to a sacred cause, a meaning so perfect, the warrior "performs the ordinary under extraordinary conditions."

In that lonely trek across my desert challenge, life became really simple. I came to understand that the test of one's caliber is what it takes to stop you. In those endless days and darkest nights, I found a few lines from the book *Endurance: Shackleton's Incredible Voyage* that transformed the hopelessness into meaningfulness. After seventeen months stranded on the Antarctic ice shelf, twenty-eight survivors made it back to civilization. While reading their journal entries, I noticed that, in some ways, they had come to know themselves better in that lonely world of ice and emptiness. They had achieved at least a limited kind of contentment. One unique entry spoke volumes. "***We'd been tested . . . and found not wanting.***" It went on to describe how they felt that special kind of pride of a person who, in a foolish moment, accepts an impossible dare—then pulls it off to perfection.

This secret that I've shared with you can carry you through life's impossible missions. It begins with a commitment to principle, to a code, that dishonoring scares you shitless. The agony that you'll suffer during your commitment must torture your soul less than standing in front of the ultimate tribunal to account for your conduct under duress.

But beyond that commitment to purpose and principle, you must possess something called passion. In my case, that passion was the fatherly love for my children. In my mind, again and again, two films replayed. One, my children standing over my headstone that they'd chosen, "Here lies an average man, like everyone else." And the other, just one word. "Worthy."

Passion fueled this father's trek across hell. It was about being scared shitless to account to my children that I'd cowered to the bully called fate and dishonored them by my fear. This fueled me to rise just one more time and trust the Creator that only through being scared shitless can we be *tested . . . and found not wanting.*

## BIOGRAPHY

As a human that has intimately danced with tragedy, injustice, and anguish, Steve lives to inspire the few destined to impact the many. He's director of performance for Success Publishing where he coaches authors inside his best friend's Mastermind group to "embrace the suck" by expressing courageous vulnerability in telling their Stories.

Mission: To deliberately cause affirmative outcomes that would not have occurred otherwise

Slogan: *Chance favors the prepared*
Mantra: No one left behind

Connect with Steve via LinkTree: https://linktr.ee/steve_moreland

CHAPTER 4

# Pause, Think And Stay Authentic

*By Amy Ruzicka*

The dramatic rescue. The common thread. The conformity. The world has a way of dictating your every move. Whether we choose our mentors or parents, we all get thrown into the pool of adulthood, naked. With different bodies, stories, and scars hiding beneath the water, we see only each other's faces. Staring, without saying a word. Staring, waiting for someone to say something. We float around interacting with those closest because it's effortless. As we gain more trust, we unknowingly feel comfortable enough to get out of the pool, dry off, and explore this life with those we've entrusted.

    I was raised in a household that appeared unbroken on the surface—that typical suburban life. My family moved around a bit. Between each household, my family had the things that make you feel successful. The pool, the Porsche, the ballet classes, and vacations, amongst other things. I am fortunate to have had supportive parents, wanting the best for my brothers and me. They always told us that we could be whatever we set our minds to. They also said that we could choose any career; whatever career we chose, we would have to strive to be the best.

    I have a lot of respect for my parents and took every word of theirs seriously. I listened and believed. I worked to be liked by all. The world has a way of showing us that we are different. So many interactions that I have had with others made me feel like I didn't fit in. I was not black enough, or skinny enough, or rich enough. The list went on and on. Within all this, I still had friends—friends from all walks of life. I had a life that most would think they want.

I never understood why I felt a space in my soul that needed to be filled, to be accepted—an area where I did not disappoint anyone and did not have something to prove. Then 2008 came, and I followed in the footsteps society expected of me. I applied to college. I wanted to be the number one modern ballerina. After an audition, I would make multiple cuts. When the final selection came in, I anxiously waited for my number or last name to be called. And then . . . silence. I left defeated! I knew I had to explore something else. I was always very gifted with science; I had talked about becoming a pediatrician from a young age. So I said, "why not?" I sent my application to multiple schools and got accepted into none of my top schools. I felt pretty unwanted but had no idea what to do with life. So I applied to a few more easy-to-get-into schools. I got into all of them and even got a small scholarship for one.

I chose the college that was far from home. I wanted freedom from the challenges my family was going through. I wanted to learn what my purpose in life was and gain a sense of community and establish new roots. Little did I know, I jumped into the deep end of the pool and could see only everyone's face. My vibrant personality and need to fit in allowed me to make friends quickly and easily. I also was naive and did not understand that the world wanted me to conform and get consumed. I joined a sisterhood with aspirations of creating my own best friends. I quickly went from a 4.0 GPA in Fall 2008 to under 1.0 GPA in Spring 2009. I even got in trouble with the law.

Suddenly, I felt that I came out of the pool alone, with no clothes, no purpose, and everyone was staring without knowing what was beneath the surface. I had to decide immediately what to do next. My parents were in the process of separation at the time. I used my parents' struggle as an excuse to start over. I left my four-year college, worked full time, and attended community college while living at home.

I started dancing and performing again. I surrounded myself with people that had similar goals and aspirations. I began to feel what joy and belonging was. I was trying to rewrite my script and bury the truth. I found myself having an internal battle to do more. I listened to the tug and applied to a four-year university. I sent in my application to Towson University as a biology major and got accepted. I decided to choose to learn about one of my gifts: science. Science has always come easily to me, and I thought, 'Why not?'. The following years involved simultaneously balancing full-time work as a pharmacy technician and fifteen or more credit hour semesters. As my senior year was approaching, I was faced with another life decision: Be done with education or keep going?

I felt that the world and all those around me were going to professional school. Again, I said, 'Why not?'. If you are reading this now, you may have some confusion if you've heard me tell my story before. The truth is, I am just now understanding who I am amid many valleys with steep mountains. At this time, I was still in the deep end of the pool, just looking at the surface of everyone and everything. I hadn't figured a way out. I was lost, and my coping mechanism made me follow the herd.

I followed what life told me to do. It told me to continue, to be more educated. You can't be successful without an education, a home, a car, a family, and so on. So, I did it. I got my doctorate in optometry, got married, completed an optional residency in ocular disease, bought a home, got a new car, checking my list off one by one. Checking my list gave me a sense of purpose, a sense of dignity. But as life came knocking on my door, I was still naked under the water, looking for a place to fit in.

The feeling of purpose came to me one day. That day, I had goosebumps on my skin as the cold, arid air brushed my cheek. I sat in a room with five girls—five strangers that I allowed in. I let them know my story, the real story. As I quaintly heard their unfamiliar voices that sounded familiar. This brought tears to my eyes, brought me joy, and I was pulled out of the water. I felt at home. There's something about laying your heart out to strangers and letting them harness it with compassion. There's something about supporting someone else's heart. I was able to see without fear, hear through the silence, and feel the light.

My purpose was staring at me in the face.

What do you see when you look at yourself?

My reflection reminds me that I do not need to fit in. The world, the internet, society, and just about everyone has an agenda for us. Achieving your most significant potential lies in your reflection, not in anyone else's. You have the power of attaining greatness when you stop listening to the norms of the world.

The checklist will teach you grit, so do it. The list does not define you. It is merely a line-by-line guidance of what to do next, not a summation of who you are and what your impact should be. I now am a residency-trained optometrist who focuses on entrepreneurship, wellness mentorship, and authorship. I write my own script. I still have valleys and mountains to climb.

Today, most people talk to me and judge me on my surface. They ask me about my demographics: whether I'm married, American, have kids, etc. I used to let these questions get under my skin because of feminism, the Black Lives Matter movement, Trump 2020, and everything else that's happening in the world. But guess what? I don't.

Do you let others dictate how you feel?

Okay, so you are allowed to have an initial feeling or thought. My ask is that you immediately discard it. You know who you are. You know your ability. You have it in you, just like I do. The moment I stopped letting others dictate how I should feel, who I should marry, what I should eat, and how many kids I should have, I began to experience inner peace and joy.

You have the power to write your own script. Stop letting individuals like Mark Zuckerberg, Jeff Bezos, or even an election, dictate your story. The moment you stop fitting in is the moment you get to unlock the key to your future. When you stop trying to do what the world asks, you begin to learn its phases. There will be many learning curves of knowing who you are because, c'mon, you've been told for how long who you are? And now you are trying to figure this out on your own. Trust me . . . It will take time. It will take grit. It will take empathy.

'You can achieve anything you put your mind to' sounds cliche. But it is so real. So now the moment of truth. How do you do this? How did I do this?

**Step 1: Say Yes to You!**

This starts with saying 'No' to others. Stop people-pleasing. You say yes to what brings you closer to inner peace and joy. If working that extra shift is just to please your boss, then say no. If working all night will bring you one step closer to your freedom, then go for it. Go for it, and don't stop. Don't be afraid to ask for help. Be raw and honest; if you don't, you are only lying to yourself.

**Step 2: Protect**

You know that feeling when you sit on a plane before take-off when they review what to do during an emergency? If you remember, taking care of yourself is essential for the passenger's survival next to you. Well, it is true. It's nearly impossible to achieve without self-care. Supply the appropriate nutrients and know your physical needs: sleep, food, and fitness. Your optimal performance comes out when your body is ready. Protect the one machine you have control over, you!

**Step 3: Support**

The moment you start supporting other humans and showing compassion, you will begin to see how fulfilling life can be. Most think life is all about glam and likes. Sure, those things make us feel temporarily happy. However, it is not until we can create genuine relationships that we see the fruits of our labor.

These three steps are the building blocks that get me through my valleys. I will not stop climbing the steep mountain. I have been able to stop hiding beneath the water, naked amongst strangers, and ascend my mountain. I know that you can do the same by saying yes to yourself, protecting yourself, and supporting others.

My next chapter may look different, but my path is the same. My course is to continue to maintain inner peace and joy. I will not stray off my path for anyone. What comes my way will look different every day. However, I will attack it the same. I will always be ready to show up, say yes to myself and support the stranger next to me. I no longer am naked, alone, hiding beneath the surface of the pool. I am no longer conforming. I am saying yes to myself. Come and join me.

## BIOGRAPHY

Amy Ruzicka is a grit-driven mentor and optometrist. Her hyperfocused attitude on individualized solutions for her clients and patients is her playbook. She recently completed a 'Woman in Leadership' certification from Cornell University. Preceding this, she completed nine years of education and residency. She enjoys being outdoors and spending time with her family. Amy's passion is to inspire others to experience the fruit that life has in store for them.

Contact Amy Ruzicka via https://linktr.ee/amyruzicka

CHAPTER 5

# There's No Such Thing As Failure

*By Anthony Pierre*

As I lay there in a jail cell, exhausted from a series of events that took place the previous night of March 3, 2009, all I could think about was my four beautiful children. I pictured their anticipation for the weekend to come, speaking among themselves and wondering what I was planning for them. In one accord, they all said with excitement: 'Blockbuster Movies!' They enjoyed having friends over for movie night and camping out in front of the big screen. As that day drew near, I pictured my ex-wife and my youngest daughter's mom making up some excuse that they couldn't come to visit me this weekend. My heart became heavy as I saw the disappointment on their faces. No parent wants to let their children down or fail to provide for their needs. I lay there feeling sad, discouraged, scared, and thinking my whole life was over. My head pounded continuously as anxiety set in, and a sense of hopelessness overwhelmed my spirit. I seriously desired a mulligan.

I believe family is one of the most important blessings to cherish. As the Bible mentions: "Lo, children are a heritage of Jehovah; And the fruit of the womb is his reward" (Ps 127:3 ASV). No child ever asks to come into this crazy world, but when they do arrive, they kick the door down, smile, and shower us with joy, happiness, and love. So, as those thoughts filled my heart at that moment, I felt a prodigious amount of guilt, frustration, anger, and animosity. I hated the fact that I had put myself in prison due to my selfishness.

I was blessed to have the pleasure of raising my oldest daughter, Courtney, since she was two years old. She's now sixteen, an A student, very smart, can sing, dance, and play the violin. Two weeks ago, I put her soon-to-be car in the shop to be custom painted with a color she picked out. I could only imagine her disappointment when she'd realize that I wouldn't be coming home anytime soon. Then, I thought of my two precious sons: Anthony, aged ten, and Aidan, aged eight. I'd been coaching them in football and basketball since they were very young, teaching them good sportsmanship, discipline, determination, and hard work. Now, instead of watching them play under the lights on Friday nights, I would only be able to offer them words of wisdom and penitentiary insights.

My mind was racing as I reminisced on all the precious time spent with my youngest daughter, Amyah, my little butterfly, who I just adore and would truly miss. We spent lots of time at the mall, Chucky Cheese, and on the park swings. She is so precious, and all I could see was her beautiful smile. I always vowed that I would be there for my children, no matter what happened in my relationships. However, now I felt like I failed them, their moms, my family, and my significant other. Never having had any real trouble with the law, not even having had a juvenile record, I was now facing twenty-two years in prison. How could I have allowed something like this to happen?

As I was thinking about all these things, I heard a female voice over an intercom in my jail cell, and she called my name: "Tony, Tony. Are you okay?" I replied, "Who are you?" She responded, "It's me. Your baby's momma." Now, I was really embarrassed. I forgot that Amyah's mom was a correctional officer in the county jail. Now, I really wanted to put my head in the sand. The questions began . . .

After my youngest daughter's mom reassured me that I was a great father and that I mattered, I felt much better. At the same time, she promised me that she would make sure my daughter had a relationship with me, no matter where I was. I felt truly blessed and appreciated by the encouragement. So, as more friends and family reached out to encourage and support me, it became clear that I was far from failure. I have always taken responsibility for my actions. When the prosecutor's attorney asked me to snitch on my friends and offered me community service (probation), I kindly refused.

Now, some may think that I'm crazy for not having taken the offer, but ask yourself: how many families are you willing to ruin just for your freedom? No one forced me to take that trip to Chicago and pick up that bag of illegal drugs. So, why would I ruin another man's life and have him separated from his family when I was the one who got caught? To each his own, but I could not do that. Maybe my mistake could have moved him to change his life. But I selfishly made that decision, and not once did I think about my family and kids. All I thought about was the money owed to me and the extra money I would make if I were successful. I arrogantly thought to myself, 'Who would stop me? I am a legitimate, successful businessman, who often comes to Chicago for real estate affairs. The police don't know who I am.' So I thought.

I nearly died when I saw those red lights flashing behind me, even though I did not commit any traffic violations. I was riding cruise control at sixty miles an hour, and my passenger, who had no clue about what was in the truck, was already screaming, 'I hate crooked cops.' I thought they were pulling me over for no reason until I saw the marked car pull up with another cruiser with a canine in it. Let the illegal search begin . . .

Now reality started to set in. As I was in the back of the car telling every lie I could think of, with hopes I could somehow get myself out of this mess, I knew that they illegally stopped me and violated my rights and the Fourth Amendment.

See, I quickly learned then that you couldn't win against an illegal system that broke the law to uphold the law. As insane as that sounds, it's the bold truth about the American legal system and its police force. And no one can deny the blatant disrespect that police officers show for black lives all over the US.

After seven months of fighting my case, I took the plea deal for six years, even though I wanted to continue fighting them. At some point, I realized that it was not worth the risk of twenty-two years, and I decided to take responsibility for my actions and started working on myself spiritually, mentally, morally, and physically. And soon, I would be free while my children were still young.

Now, as I was riding on the bus headed to the CRC (Correctional Reception Center), I was chained together, both my wrists and feet, with two other men, one to my right and the other one to my left. I couldn't help but reflect on my life as I was being smashed between two grown men. I began to think to myself, 'I was a successful high school football player. In college, I earned a football scholarship and graduated from Western Illinois University with a BA. Right out of college, in 1998, I helped build ACE Mortgage Company, the first minority-owned, HUD-approved mortgage lender in Indiana, Kentucky, and Ohio, as we used our resources to empower and change many lives in our community. In 2001, I started Mactone Investments Inc., and I became a successful real estate investor. I started out with no money and bought seventeen houses in less than six months owning over 2.2 million in real estate in a blink of an eye. However, as this bumpy ride continued, my mind went back and forth, raising the question again: am I a failure?

As we finally approached our destination, my mind continued to jog around that big question. Nevertheless, we were locked down for twenty-three hours a day, so I could not help but think even deeper and raised another question: 'There is no such thing as failure, is there? Do we really fail when unfortunate things happen to us? Whether our own doing or via unforeseen circumstances? We all make mistakes, but does that make us all failures? I had to sit back and really think about this because all through our lives, we are told that we should not be failures, but yet, we all fail at something. No one is perfect. For example, an influential billionaire businessman who has been married five times or a famous female singer who is a drug addict. They are both successful in their respective fields but have struggled in other areas of life. Does this make them failures?

Do any of these factors make us failures? Let's dig deeper. What is failure? The dictionary states: "Lack of success. An unsuccessful person, enterprise or, thing." To me, that sounds like a permanent condition and maybe one reason we all have a hard time seeing ourselves as successful despite our many mistakes, shortcomings, or letdowns. Failure is so powerful that it can control your life despite all your successes and become a vacuum, sucking the life out of all your achievements.

We are what we think. So, if we think we are failures, guess what? We *are* failures. So that's why, today, I am challenging the word. Even the most sacred and most popularly sold book, the Bible, does not call us failures. God never uses the word failure in the entire Bible. Wow! So, even our Creator does not see us as failures, so why should we? In reality, as I lay in my cell thinking, I decided to self-affirm, 'There is no such thing as failure.' After convincing my heart, I instantly felt power and joy come over me even though I still had 1,980 days left in prison. However, I was very optimistic as to what the future held.

John Keats once said, "Don't be discouraged by a failure. It can be a positive experience. Failure is, in a sense, the highway to success, inasmuch as every discovery of what is false leads us to seek earnestly after what is true, and every fresh experience points out some form of error which we shall afterwards carefully avoid."[1] Amazing wisdom from a young poet who died of tuberculosis at the age of twenty-five. He was so young, brilliant, and full of promise. Although his life was cut short, he left us with an amazing insight on the topic of failure. As I read his story, I could only reminisce and think about my own life at the young age of twenty-five. Looking back, I must say, I was so blessed because I had seen things and been places, and I have four beautiful children who love me.

So, I believe **there is no such thing as failure** and that we must look at our lives as a series of events and stages that foster growth in our weaknesses. We all make errors, but if we look at life from a positive perspective, there's nothing that can bar us from our goals. We all stumble, but what's most important is that we keep getting back up. When I finished my 1,980 days on March 3, 2015, I had accomplished the following:

---

1  "A Quote by John Keats," Goodreads (Goodreads), accessed April 13, 2021, https://www.goodreads.com/quotes/226582-don-t-be-discouraged-by-a-failure-it-can-be-a#:~:text=It%20can%20be%20a%20positive,we%20shall%20afterwards%20carefully%20avoid.%E2%80%9D.

- baptized and became an ordained minister and one of Jehovah's Witnesses, helping many to learn about God and all his wonderful promises
- became a competent auto mechanic graduating from auto school
- passed my Water 1 and Water 2 license tests that have a forty-two percent pass rating
- created and taught one of the most successful real estate investment courses in prison through Urban University, from which thousands of students are now benefiting and changing their lives as we speak
- won three flag football championships in a row
- won two basketball championships and one runner-up

I guess that there's really no such thing as failure.

## BIOGRAPHY

Anthony Pierre's life was turned upside down when he was suddenly arrested and sent to prison for six years. While in prison, he searched deep within himself to understand who he truly was. During this crisis, he found his love for writing lost in his childhood. Anthony loves writing poetry, motivational articles, and real estate investing publications. Anthony is a successful real estate investor with more than twenty years of experience in the business. He also owns Estate Masters Real Estate Academy and a successful business in the network marketing space. Anthony has taught his secrets to hundreds while changing people's lives all over the world through public speaking, teaching life lessons, and inspiring people to change their mindset. Anthony was born and raised in Cincinnati, Ohio, where he currently lives with his wife and four children.

Contact Anthony Pierre via https://linktr.ee/Apierre1002

CHAPTER 6

# Metamorphosis Is My Story Of Becoming . . .

*By B. Heather Pinard*

I had just punched a boy in the nose. You could see how shocked everyone was that I had done such a thing. Of course, the boy's nose started to bleed, and someone handed him a handkerchief. I stood there defiantly, warning others I was ready for war, that I was not to be messed with any longer. When I did it, I knew I was going to get in trouble, but I had decided enough was enough, and I was not going to take it anymore. I didn't care if I got expelled from school or how angry my parents were going to be. In the moment, I just knew I had to do it. I was eleven years old at the time.

For years, in that and other schools I had attended, the children, and sometimes teachers, found ways to humiliate me, taunt me, tease me, and yes, even bully me. And at one point, I thought that if life was going to be like that, I did not know if I wanted to be around, just to be everyone's verbal punching bag. In this particular school, the worst culprit was the principal's daughter. She was the ringleader of all the bullying. My other classmates, though I definitely would not call them my mates, would join in with her. She kept telling me that going to the principal would not help, as her mother, the principal, would never believe her daughter could do such things; it was my word against hers, and her mother would always believe her over me. No one in school would come to my aid. They did not want to be a victim, too. Then a new family moved into the area, and our parents became fast friends. I finally developed a friendship with their daughter, who happened to be in my class. She became a witness and saw and heard all that was said and done to me. She made an attempt to step in and help me, but she soon saw no one was listening.

I was taken to the principal's office, where I proceeded to tell the principal her precious daughter was the instigator and the chief one responsible for most of the verbal bullying, teasing, and taunting directed at me. I told her I would not put up with it anymore. I explained that was why I had punched the boy in the nose—I had thought he, too, was about to sling more verbal arrows at me.

Of course, the principal didn't believe her daughter would do such things until I told her I had a witness, and by calling on others, she finally realized I was telling the truth.

She was very apologetic about her daughter's behavior, and I was not expelled under those conditions. I apologized to the boy, and life continued without any more abuse. However, shortly after that, it was decided I should attend a more international school, an idea very much to my liking.

Though I never had to deal with such problems again, the years of trauma I had suffered turned me into a very quiet, watchful child. I felt I did not come into my own until I was a senior in high school.

My situation was not unusual: Unfortunately, past statistics show that around seventy-one percent of young girls and many young men too, who attended high school in those days experienced some form of bullying, whether verbal or physical. However, these days, the figure is much worse, around eighty-three percent among girls. The increase is likely due to the rise of social media among the students. Nowadays, these young teenagers must deal with new forms of abuse, so-called cyberbullying, which can involve malicious posting on the internet of a type calculated to make the recipient suffer. This has also caused a rise in suicide rates among teenagers, as well as an increase in drug use and other damaging antisocial behaviors not conducive to their well-being.

I noticed that as life progressed, I encountered people who thought my shyness was a reason to take advantage of me. But they did not know the depths of my resolve that those days of being bullied should be over, or so I thought. Life has a way of throwing curveballs our way if we don't learn from our past experiences. It is sad to think that a high proportion of people have to go through life still suffering the effects of the trauma they experienced as children or teenagers.

To begin to deal with the underlying emotions and memories that contribute to being affected by childhood trauma, we must first understand that we are all born with our "basic" set of emotions. According to American psychologist Paul Eckman, we are born with six basic emotions: Surprise, Happiness, Anger, Sadness, Disgust, and Fear. All other emotions are offshoots of these. If you have spent enough time around babies, you will undoubtedly have witnessed all those emotions being expressed. They freely exhibit smiles, surprise, and fear. Add to those anger, if we don't pick them up soon enough; disgust, shown by the wrinkling of their nose at some food they have decided they don't like; and sadness when you leave the room.

To carry it a step further, psychologist Robert Plutckik created the 'Wheel of Emotion' (1980), which features different colors associated with various emotions. The use of color shows how emotions are sometimes blended so that primary, secondary, and third-level emotions can be easily identified.

Many years after my high school experience, I became involved with a company with a "5-fold" mission and philosophy. One of the five was a healthy mind, and, through doing exercises developed by Mr. Proffit, I was finally able to begin "the journey of me." For the first time, I was introduced to the workings of our conscious and subconscious minds and how our limiting beliefs, or programming, keep us from moving forward in our lives. I was taught how to create an empty space in my mind, so that new information could be accepted, thereby opening my mind to new thoughts and ideas. We all have such limiting beliefs, and some of us get so stuck with them that we are unable to expand our minds beyond what we already perceive. Some people even want to stay stuck. However, I was not one of them, and the training opened my mind to other possibilities, which engendered different and more positive results for me. The training was only the first step on a journey of learning about a world I wanted to know more about. In short, it helped me to see I could break out and expand my "comfort zone," learning other techniques I could utilize to take me to different levels of consciousness. In doing so, I was able to metamorphose into the person I am today. What follows is some of the knowledge imparted to me and some of the techniques I have learned that may help you, too.

Our memories are created in our subconscious mind, even as a fetus in the womb. Studies have shown the fetus in the mother's seventh month of pregnancy already has a memory. Since our subconscious does not know what is real or not, it will take everything it perceives is happening to you and around you and stores it for later use. When those experiences are put into storage, an emotion is created around them, and we give it life when we recall it.

Since the subconscious cannot determine between real and non-real experience, it sometimes builds up a "heart wall" around incidents it decides it should protect us from remembering; that is according to Dr. Bradley Nelson in his book *The Emotion Code* (2019). That is why we sometimes make our affirmations come to fruition right away, while others seem to elude us. This "heart wall" put up by the subconscious can make it difficult for us to accomplish our dreams, desires, and goals. We may have been programmed that way without our knowledge; the wall may be constructed from, say, the doings and thoughts of our parents or grandparents that happened around us while we were still in the womb. Or they could be actions or thoughts from people around our mother during pregnancy. And, as with 'blended emotions,' we must release these emotions in the correct order.

Dr. Darren Weissman, holistic physician, whose books include *The Power of Infinite Love and Gratitude* (2007) and *Awakening the Secret Code of Your Mind* (2010), used elements of the work of the Japanese scientist

Dr. Masaru Emoto that featured in his bestselling book *The Hidden Messages in Water* (2005). Masaru did Corilian light studies with water and found the two most perfect crystals found in frozen water are Love and Gratitude. He proposed that, since our bodies are seventy percent water and our minds are ninety percent water, we can change the vibration in the water by using those words. He suggested that, in our bodies and minds, there is a correlation between the vibration of our emotions and the ability of our bodies to change as we change that vibration by using the words Love and Gratitude. According to Darren Weissman, because Love and Gratitude are infinite, we can, therefore, say Infinite Love and Gratitude. He has created a hand motion using the "I Love You" sign in braille to be used in conjunction with speaking the words Infinite Love and Gratitude.

Along with this, I also learned more about Neurokenesis (the movement between the braincase and palate at the basipterygopterygoid joint), in particular a technique of handwashing that stimulates both left and right brain hemispheres simultaneously. Today, this relatively new technique is increasingly employed to treat people with brain injuries and PTSD (Post Traumatic Stress Disorder). Unsurprisingly perhaps, many of us have brain injuries despite never having been in combat. Nevertheless, some events we experience may be so traumatic, they leave an imprint on our subconscious that has a negative effect on our behavioral responses to our general detriment. An example of this is clearly visible in the most common symptoms of PTSD associated with childhood trauma. I also learned about EFT (Emotional Freedom Techniques), Tapping, and EMDR (Eye Movements Desensitizing and Reprocessing).

Additionally, I learned about access consciousness and transgenerational clearing in different forms and learning to meditate using both directed and self-directed methods. In the directed system, called Ho'Oponopo, I learned about a type of breathing and relaxation that helps rid us of what the Hawaiians call the mistakes that we and our subconscious have created to keep us stuck. And, armed with self-meditation techniques from meditation teacher Sherry Huber, I learned a different breathing technique to help me clear the negative emotions and the "cobwebs" from the past that lingered in my mind and quiet my mind and put myself at ease.

As I was learning more about my mind and how I could take control of my thoughts and emotions and, therefore, my memories, I used some of their techniques and others to advance myself and my mind to the realization that I had a choice in how I reacted to things. I could be the victim and let things happen to me, or I could be proactive and take my power back. That is what I had realized at age eleven when I was being bullied at school. Not that everything fell into place right away—it has been a journey of self-discovery of moving forward slowly. That is not to say I never fall back. After the trauma of my husband's death, I did fall back and let others take advantage of me. Since then, I have successfully gotten back on the journey and am going forward again. I now choose to think of the memories that kept me locked down as good memories, for if I did not have them, I would not have gone on my quest to be the new person that I now am. I could choose to be the victim; I could choose to be aggressive. Or I could choose to hold my own, be patient, while not being the "door-mat" I once felt I was. My hope is that those of you who are searching for ways to clear your life of drama and trauma from the past may find some of these, and other, techniques useful in becoming the new you. It is also important to remember to add fun and happy memories along your life's journey to sustain you as you make new discoveries and create new paths for yourself. I hope they will show you how you, too, can come through the tunnel and create a healing light for yourself as I have done.

## BIOGRAPHY

B. Heather Pinard has a master's degree in education and wrote educational courses before becoming an author. She is certified in applied kinesiology and the Emotion Code technique. She is also a Reiki Master. Her coauthored books include *Success from the Heart* (2015) and *Women Who Rock* (2018), both of which have become number one best-sellers. A video from her talk at Harvard Business School based on her last book, *Words that Kill, The Power of Language and Promise of Peace* (2017), can be found on her website wordsthatkillbook.com. She has spoken at different business groups, focusing on helping people achieve their "why" in life. In her spare time, she loves to paint watercolors, visit with family and friends, and travel the world.

Contact B. Heather Pinard via http://wordsthatkillbook.com

CHAPTER 7

# Don't Find An Excuse, Find A Way

*By Bobbie Hall*

Growing up with my family, we heard phrases like: "Don't find an excuse, find a way to get it done," and using the word "can't" was frowned upon because we perceived this as giving up. We were taught to show respect to our elders and people of authority (coaches, teachers, bosses, etc.) and put our entire effort into everything we did, be it schoolwork, sports, or part-time jobs. The lessons learned from my parents and my experiences have significantly impacted me and shaped who I am today. These foundational lessons taught me to value hard work and perseverance—to get me back up when I fall.

Growing up in my family, there was no shortage of activities and responsibilities. Between the schedules of two working parents and three kids, there were plenty of opportunities to learn how to deal with setbacks when the situation didn't go as planned. I borrowed this saying from a good friend of mine who also happens to coach our boys: "You either win or you learn." So really, there is no losing in life unless one chooses to give up. Setbacks are simply learning opportunities.

If you take a look at my life on paper, you might say, "Wow, you must be so proud of all that you have accomplished." Yes: high school and college sports accolades; respected alumnus and teacher at my alma mater; successful coach; a loving wife and mother of two; and running a successful networking marketing business. But, missing on that paper are all the times of struggle, failure, or what I went through behind the scenes. Often, I felt broken but would pick up the pieces and put them back together; then, I would be stronger than before.

So how did this foundation built inside of me get put to the test?

My athletic skills separated me from others throughout middle school and high school, not just on the court or field but also socially. Sometimes I felt like I was on an island, fending for myself with no one to talk to about my loneliness. Unconsciously, I built this wall in my mind and told myself that everything was fine; I didn't need help, and I could push through anything myself. This mindset worked for a while but proved to be unsustainable. I tolerated being purposely elbowed and pinched at basketball practices—this was my teammates' way of making sure I was tough enough to be on varsity. I pushed through injuries like rolled ankles, shin splints, sore muscles, stiff lower back, shoulder pain from throwing a softball so hard to get a base runner out at home plate that my arm hung as I finished the throw, and even stress fractures as a result of pushing through the pain of shin splints. This happened twice, and the second time was a breaking point for me in my college basketball career.

I felt as if I had a lot to prove in my senior year of college. I wanted to contribute on the court and behind the scenes as the exemplar team player and leader I had been for my entire career as an athlete, whether I was the star out on the field or court, or when I played a role player on a team full of studs, playing hard for the team on the field and being supportive from the bench and in the locker room behind the scenes. I trained so hard that I started the season with shin splints. Over time, they became so painful that I usually left the gym with four or five bags of ice wrapped around my legs after practice. Walking across campus to classes became painful with every step I took, and even sleeping was painful. I am not the type of leader or teammate who shies away from work. I get in there and do the work—the hard work—the kind that you pour blood, sweat, and tears into. I pushed myself so far to prove to a new coach that I could do it and earn my spot, yet the shin splints had become stress fractures and ended up benching me. I sat out much of the pre-season and our first few games until my shins began to heal. I had never been so injured that I had to sit out for that length of time. When I came back, no matter how hard I worked or how well I practiced, I felt like my ways of contributing to this team were being crushed and pushed aside. I didn't play during our last home game when teams usually start their seniors or, at least, get them in the game for a few minutes. My entire family (grandparents, aunts, uncles, cousins, siblings, parents, and fiancé) was watching, and for me not to deliver, to fail, was heartbreaking. Never had I felt this low in my athletic career, or ever in my life. As an athlete who prides herself on a strong work ethic, commitment to the team, a great attitude, and integrity, this crushed me. This was not how I pictured my athletic career coming to an ending.

I didn't ask or plan to get hurt, and for a long time, I questioned: "Why me?" But this happened because I was more worried about proving myself to a coach, rather than listening to my body. I just kept telling myself that the pain was short-term, and I would be fine—that I needed to just push through it. Look where that got me. I was so stubborn and determined to succeed because someone told me I couldn't, and I became so focused on getting better that I missed the signs telling me that I needed to back off. So, on top of feeling like I failed athletically, I was also feeling guilty for ignoring my pain and not speaking up sooner.

After all of my years of playing and coaching sports, I have concluded that many great life lessons can be learned from athletics. Win with integrity and character, but also learn from the losses. This situation may have broken my heart, but it also opened my eyes. No matter the successes or failures I've had in my life, I can always thank my athletic experiences and the lessons my dad instilled in me along the way.

My dad had always found the right words to say. After that game, he said: "Yeah, this really sucks, but you can always learn something from every situation—good or bad—and from every leader or person of authority you work with or play for. You can learn what to do and what not to do. So, what did you learn from this?" What did I learn? I had learned to listen to my body more attentively. I realized no matter how much hard work I'd put in, or how good I am at something, I may not always please everyone. But as long as I know I worked hard and smart, that'd be all I could ask from myself. I learned that I could not control what others thought or did. I learned to listen to my students and players that I would one day teach and coach, and not assume the worst because they weren't meeting my expectations. Sometimes, things happen in the background, of which we are not aware, but we don't know unless we listen. I learned that failure is not the end result, but simply a step toward mastery. I learned that a broken heart is not the end, but a chance to start something new. I learned that I am not defined by my abilities, but by my character, and how I respond in times of adversity shows my true character.

I have "lost" many times in sports and my professional career. I often felt failure as an athlete, mom, teacher, coach, and in building my network-marketing business; and some of those losses had me on the ropes, questioning whether or not I was cut out for the task at hand.

As a mom, I feel pride when my boys demonstrate that work ethic and have confidence and excitement to try something new or show me what they have been practicing. However, there were days when I compared myself to other moms and would tell myself that I was not as good as they were, and I wondered if I was failing my kids. Yet, when I felt like this, my boys always seemed to be more snuggly and tell me that I was the best mom ever. As a teacher and a former coach, there are days when I question my purpose in these jobs. Then a student sends me an email thanking me for helping them get through their strenuous day. In my network-marketing business, I have built my organization to the fifth rank out of nine in our company—even though people quit, stopped enrolling, stopped working, and chunks of my organization dwindled. But I keep going and rebuilding because there is always someone who reaches out to me for help through this business and I know I am changing lives for the better. Even on the toughest days, I don't give up; I WON'T give up. Why? Because my purpose is to be the best mom, teacher, and leader I can be for others. I want to change lives for the better.

The difference between success and failure is how many times one gets back up. We all face and experience failures, obstacles, and setbacks in life, but only those who "get back up" will continue to learn and grow. We can either live life making one excuse after another for why we didn't win, or even shift blame to someone else for our failures, or we can take ownership of the situation and responsibility for our own actions; we can seek solutions. In every situation, we have the ability to respond in a way that either helps us grow through each experience or curl up in a ball and give up. We must simply make a choice to grow and learn.

I have undergone a lot of personal development focusing on my mindset and growing in my faith, and I now understand that I can pick and choose the thoughts that enter my mind; and the thoughts I take to heart truly matter. I put in much work to change my mindset from "I am not good enough," and "What's my purpose?" to "I am making a difference," and "My purpose is to serve the greater good." All those times my dad said, "Don't find an excuse, find a way," and "'Can't' should not be in your vocabulary," was the foundation for this shift. As much as I fought it when I was a teenager, my dad was right. Choosing to be miserable and preferring to blame others for our faults or failures, those are just excuses blocking us from our greatness.

I love teaching and coaching, but I haven't always felt fulfilled, so I started searching for a greater purpose. I took it a little further and began my own network-marketing business with a great health and wellness company because it challenged me to grow as a person, and it aligns with my values and drive to help others. Co-authoring this book is another piece of the puzzle to building greater purpose. But what if I had given up and quit before I realized my goal? What if I chose not to work on my mindset or grow my faith? What if I chose not to start a business? What if I decided not to be a teacher? What if I quit sports when I was injured, struck out, or missed a shot? Well, I don't want to think about where I might have been in life if I had given up. Some might call me an eternal optimist, always full of positivity. I see myself as someone strong enough to overcome obstacles and persevere through difficult times. Not everything is always good, but I can see the good in everything. I have dreams for myself and my family, and nothing will stand in the way of those dreams coming true. I want to leave you with a final quote by John Dewey: "The self is not something ready-made; but something in continuous formation through choice of action."[2] You get to choose whether or not you get back up, so I challenge you to dig deep and find a reason to get back up, fight for your dreams, and find your greater purpose. Don't give up on yourself; you'll thank yourself later.

## BIOGRAPHY

Bobbie Hall is an inspirational high school Health and Physical Education teacher, a mompreneur, happily married to Jeff (2005), and they are blessed with two beautiful boys. She is passionate about working toward overall health and wellness through clean living and creating a positive mindset while empowering others to do the same. What sets her apart from others is her determination and perseverance in overcoming obstacles. Her experience playing two division 1 college sports, 10+ years of coaching high school sports, 14 years of teaching, and completing her Registered Yoga Teacher (RYT 200) certification have played a role in shaping her grit and mindset today. No matter the obstacles that come her way, Bobbie continues to encourage hundreds of students and families to put their health and wellness first. Her mission in teaching and in business is to empower others to become the best version of themselves.

Contact Bobbie Hall via https://linktr.ee/BobbieHall

---

2   Bodhipaksa, "John Dewey: 'The Self Is Not Something Ready-Made, but Something in Continuous Formation through Choice of Action.'," Wildmind, November 11, 2010, https://www.wildmind.org/blogs/quote-of-the-month/john-dewey-the-self-is-not-something-ready-made.

CHAPTER 8

# What Is Your True Purpose?

*By David Minshall*

Have you ever looked in the mirror and asked, "Who am I?" Waxing metaphysical, did you ever ask, "How was I created?" The purpose of this chapter is to shed a little light on who you are, how to be your best self, and discovering what your true purpose is in this world.

My self-perception (identity) when I see myself in the mirror is of a forty-six-year-old white male, short of stature, and a little bit round in the middle, calling myself a chubby little hobbit. When I delve a little deeper, I look at the good and the bad. My positive attributes: I'm funny, social, affectionate, driven, I have faith in God, I'm a good physical therapist, and I have a desire for self-improvement. My negative attributes: I frequently complain, lay blame, act as a victim, over-indulgent in food and finances, over-extend myself in projects, and think being a workaholic is a badge of honor.

**HOW DID I GET HERE?**

As a child, I felt well-provided for. Still, in our authoritarian Christian home, my perception was that we experienced frequent corporal punishments, yelling, fighting, and a general lack of affection and quality time spent together. As a coping mechanism, I would spend much of my time in my room with my door closed, keeping quiet, and reducing my interactions. I looked toward sports, academic achievement, and working to bolster my self-worth through external validation. It wasn't all bad; obviously, my parents loved me, and there were good times, but, like many of us, I learned to focus on the negative at a young age.

During my second half of college, I met my first wife, and we had some good years but then drifted apart. We had our separate roles, working and raising the kids, but eventually, we divorced. I have always worked between two to four jobs throughout most of my working career, working up to seventy-five hours a week in the physical therapy field. My perception was that I needed to work to provide for my family and keep up with my overspending, which I used as a coping mechanism for my difficult situation.

As a young adult and right up until recently, instead of dealing with the pain of emotional detachment and lack of affection directly, I acted the same as when I was a child, resorting to being avoidant, angry, and resentful. I considered myself a victim, which became the lens through which I viewed my relationships and, to a lesser extent, my work environments when I felt I had been wronged. I felt I was justified in my victimhood because others had mistreated me. I was right, and they were wrong. I was just reacting to how they treated me. And I would hold onto my grudge because they were at fault, not me. Why forgive them when they were the ones causing the pain? I would continue to complain and lay blame for how unfair life is.

I was blind to the fact that I had a perceptual problem. One, I may not have seen the situation clearly, and two, I did not realize that not forgiving my supposed offender was quite harmful to me, as well. Unbeknownst to me, becoming a victim who complained, blamed, and did not forgive others had become central to my character and identity. Through every supposed wrong done to me, I created prison walls around my heart and my mind to protect myself from being hurt further. In the deep recesses of this prison, I nurtured my pain and suffering and avoided resolution—because I knew I was right. Or was I? Was it just a prideful perception that I thought I was right? However, right I was in my prison, I was still alone, angry, and resentful.

I judged injustices quickly and failed to see that I was in the wrong by harboring pain and unforgiveness (Matthew 7:1-5).[3] For nearly thirty-five years, I have lived like an immature child in an invisible prison that I unknowingly fortified with anger, resentment, and conflict avoidance. I have not dealt with these issues much and have carried them from relationship to relationship. Through writing this chapter and thoroughly examining my life, my mind, my heart, and my spirit, I realize my lack of awareness of these problems and lack of forgiveness for myself and others has stood in the way of me living life to my fullest potential and true to my purpose (1 Peter 4:10).[4] I was so busy in the trap of working seventy plus hours a week and spending all the money I earned and more, I was too tired to figure out how to improve my life. But I would get nudges from God that told me a better life awaited.

Through prayer, scripture, and research, I found we suffer this painful journey for a reason. Vishen Lakhiani of Mindvalley said it perfectly: "Your pain is often the breadcrumbs to your values and those values become the guiding light for your purpose on the planet. Because, what often happens is that the pain gives us a glimpse of what we want to heal and fix in the world."[5] I discovered my core values of growth, love, and forgiveness, which would form the light to help others discover their True Purpose.

Today, I took action and started on my journey of forgiveness. First, praying to God to forgive me for holding onto my pain, anger, and resentment (Ephesians 4:31).[6] I asked for strength, humility, and not being prideful in counting the wrongs people have done me (James 5:6-12).[7] Instead, I made a list of those whom I felt I had wronged or those

---

3   Mt 7:1-5

4   1 Pt 4:10

5   Mindvalley Talks, "How to Find Your Contribution to the World Today | Vishen Lakhiani," *YouTube* video, 49:23, January 30, 2020, https://www.youtube.com/watch?v=SBuA_XjnEmY&feature=emb_logo.

6   Eph 4:31

7   Jas 5:6-12

against whom I held a grudge because I thought they had wronged me. I reviewed the lens that I was looking through during the situation and tried to put myself in the other person's shoes to understand their perspective. I reached out to a few of them and apologized for my part in making the situation difficult (Ephesians 4:32).[8] Three of them responded, and we reconciled.

Recently, I have been researching forgiveness and love. Forgiveness and love go hand and hand (1 Corinthians 13:4-7).[9] I wanted to heal my heart, mind, body, and spirit from the years of damage done by the anger and resentment I had held onto. I knew deep down that my personality or current identity (my default self) did not work anymore and could not fix my problems. Almost every important area of my life, health, wealth, spirituality, and emotional wellbeing was lacking. What stood out to me the most was forgiveness and the concept of unconditional love. I discovered I needed to learn how to love others whom I care for in my life unconditionally, meaning I love and accept them for who they are, where they are at, and not who I want them to be. The more expectations or conditions that we put on love, the more we will be disappointed. Relationships are not meant to be a calculation of wrongs and rights, black and white, but are about loving the other person in their entirety and enjoying them, even in the gray areas. Once we step out of our own narrative of how we think our loved ones should be, we are free to enjoy them for who they are. We can only change ourselves. We can become increasingly happy by leading with love, kindness, and support instead of anger, resentment, and coldness. It doesn't mean we're a doormat for toxic behavior or without boundaries; it means we learn to be more creative in interacting with each other in a positive manner.

For my personal healing and transformation, I needed to root out my broken identity to carry out my True Purpose. The realization that I had built my own prison of pain, anger, and resentment to avoid future hurt was the first key to breaking free and becoming my true self.

---

8   Eph 4:32
9   1 Cor 13:4-7

God forged me through my negative perception, trials, and suffering to prepare me for the meaningful work of helping others. Viktor Frankl said it best: "In some way, suffering ceases to be suffering the moment it finds a meaning, such as the meaning of a sacrifice."[10] The second key was realizing my perception that people had done me injustice and my negative reaction to protect myself. My self-narrative is not how the world truly is, just the lens I see it through. Other lenses are different, but I didn't stop to consider that. In my transformation into my newer and stronger identity, I am no longer a victim with a poor mindset and self-limiting beliefs, like the universe is out to get me. When frustration approaches, I examine how I can be the solution versus going straight to anger or complaint. The third key to breaking free is walking the path of forgiveness and unconditional love for myself and others, just as God does for me. My source of significance and power comes from my relationship with God and those around me. With these three keys coming together, I started my journey in discovering my TRUE Purpose.

- What personal prison do you live in? Why?
- Do you have a negative or positive lens you view the world through?
- Do you live as a victim or take personal responsibility for your life and your choices? How can you change for the better?
- Forgive yourself and others any grudges to free yourself. Pick a couple of people you can connect with and forgive them.
- What did you think of the concept of unconditional love and accepting people for who they are?
- Write down a couple of ways to have a heart of forgiveness and unconditional love in your life. Do you think that will allow you to be a happier person?

---

10  8 Key Learnings from Man's Search for Meaning by Viktor Frankl — Wealth of Happiness, 2021

## HOW TO FIND YOUR TRUE PURPOSE

You may or may not believe in God, but through my research in the bible, other sources, and prayer, I have discovered some clues that are useful in finding our True Purpose.

1. We are sent here for a purpose; I believe you are called by God (Matthew 4:18-20)[11] to deliver your unique gift to the world for a better society (Proverbs 18:16).[12] Sharing our gifts improves the world.

2. We are pre-packaged with our unique gift inside of us (1 Peter 4:11),[13] where we can find it easily (just like an apple seed holds the apple tree inside but does not grow until it is put in soil and fertilized).

3. Your unique gift is what you are good at and enjoy, acknowledges God, and helps your neighbor (Romans 12:6).[14]

4. Do a timeline for the bad times in your life. Study the bad; we are forged in this life for a reason, to handle the stresses and pressures of what life is going to throw at us so that we can be a positive force for the greater good. God does not give you what you cannot handle.

5. Do a timeline for the good in your life. Reflect when you felt on fire, doing something wonderful that you enjoyed and felt good at. Look closely at these times, as they will shed light on your gift.

6. Pray or meditate over your gift every day, as well as work on your self-development. You will see glimpses of God guiding you in the right direction (Matthew 7:7-11).[15]

---

11   Mt 4:18-20
12   Prv 18:16
13   1 Pt 4:11
14   Rom 12:6
15   Mt 7:7-11

7. Start with what you can handle; don't quit your job right away. Even the Apostle Paul was a tentmaker to pay the bills.

8. Now you have your newfound gift, give it away for free at first. God and people will reward you in the end. It takes a while to cultivate a gift and create value for others. They will pay you well for your fruit (apples) that began from the seed inside you. Your gift (fruit/apple) is for others to consume. An apple tree does not consume its own fruit.

Writing this chapter has finally given me pause to grow closer to God, discover my TRUE Purpose, and reduce others' suffering and help them discover their TRUE Purpose.

## BIOGRAPHY

David Minshall is an orthopedic physical therapist. He holds a Six Sigma Green Belt in Efficiency. He is an email copywriter, a network marketer, and a transformer (not the robot kind!). He has written poetry and was placed in a philosophy writing competition. As a recovering workaholic and pessimist, he relied on complaining, blaming, and a negative mindset to FAIL through his day. He traded in his old and broken ways and began his journey of Transformation. Under God's guidance, he is dedicated to the practice of forgiveness, positive mindset, personal growth, and unconditional love. His mission is to share the knowledge that God and the Universe are working for us abundantly and not against us in scarcity. He proclaims everyone was put on earth on purpose and to share a True Purpose. His passions are volunteering, personal development, spending time with friends and family, gold panning, and fishing in his backyard on Kodiak Island, Alaska.

Contact David Minshall at https://linktr.ee/davidminshall

CHAPTER 9

# Just Keep Pushing

*By Denver Duncan*

My name is Denver Duncan. I'm from a tiny town in Wisconsin. All my life, I felt like I was meant to impact the world somehow in some way but wasn't quite sure of the means to do so. I remember one day in school looking out the window at a furniture factory where it seemed like everyone, at one point or another, went to work, and I thought: this cannot be life. I know I didn't get the best grades, but this couldn't be it. I had three options: go to school, get a job, or join the military. I ended up taking the military route and joined the Army. So right after high school, while everyone else was celebrating their freedom, I was doing pushups at boot camp with a duffle bag on my back, with another bag on my front side which had to be flat when my chest hit the ground while doing pushups.

While serving in the Army—and I'm sure the other branches did this too—if your uniform wasn't pressed, or your boots weren't shined up enough, then the sergeants made you do pushups as a reminder to get yourself taken care of (squared away for the vets). You see, when you look like a soldier, you will think like a soldier, and you will become a soldier. And if you didn't, you had to do pushups along with other exercises to remind you to get squared up. The sergeants would say: 'Just keep on pushing until I get tired of you doing pushups.' It was then that I had to learn how to speedily shine the boots to almost look like mirrors on my feet and press my uniform exceptionally well. I had learned these lessons well because my sergeants drilled them into my head till they became second nature—tasks like first aid and field stripping your weapon and putting it back together. In the meanwhile, you'd explain it back to the sergeants so they could either give you a passing grade or make you do it all over again. After all, when you were done with those tasks, it was up to you to train your troops on how to get the job done; when it was correctly done, your mission would be accomplished. Now, if there was any piece of the puzzle missing, it could've been disastrous.

Years later, I had retired from the Army and transitioned over to civilian lifestyle. It had its challenges, but hey, who doesn't like to be challenged, right? I know what you are thinking: how can this help me out? That's a good question. You see, in the military, we had life and death situations that could occur at any time, and we had to maintain a certain attitude, be able to adapt to what seemed like last-minute changes, and overcome the situation to make the mission a success. It goes the same way with the civilian world and business. If you don't know what you are doing and you've not squared away, and if you are dealing with a client, or a prospect, or even your boss, guess what's going to happen? The client will more than likely back out of the deal and go with someone else; your staff or coworkers won't be able to meet your demands and deadlines. Your boss will go in on you and give you some sort of counseling, or worse, terminate you for poor performance. So if you don't know what is going on or having a hard time understanding something, there is absolutely nothing wrong with asking for help. It is better than saying 'Yeah, I know,' and then have everything fall apart.

Now, to get through all of this, you need to have a good attitude—one that can help you clearly see the task at hand. In the military, we called this attitude 'getting your mind right and tightening up your shot group, so you can just keep pushing.' There will be people and challenges in the way of your pursuits. Some of them want to see you get emotional, quit early, and be happy with just what you got. Why go through the hassle because you're not smart enough, not good-looking, or you do not have enough experience to be able to get the job done? What happens next?

You know that stuff they tell you about yourself isn't true. But because they are like your family and friends, it hurts a bit. So, you start thinking to yourself that this can all be done another day and another time. Time goes by and nothing gets done. Even as I write this, I'm getting all kinds of negativity from everyone I know, ranging from 'Why are you doing this crap?' to 'You don't even read books and here you are writing one,' or 'Why can't you just be happy with your job?' You get the picture, I hope! How do we turn these negative, hurtful comments into commendations? Keep on pushing through the rest of this and we can find those answers together!

 Remember all those statements you heard when you were just a little kid growing up? Statements like "Whether you can, or you can't, you're right" and "If you hesitate, you lose." I used to think that was stupid, but now, later in life, it does mean something. "If you can put your mind to it, you can accomplish anything." Now that's true because if you are genuinely passionate about something, you can make it happen. I like professional wrestling; it has a certain entertainment value to it. Yes, I know that it is all choreographed. However, things do happen. The reason why I watch it is because the wrestlers trash-talking each other is pretty funny stuff. Most of the time, these wrestlers just trash talk. But every once in a while, they do spit out a bit of truth. My bit of truth is this quote from one wrestler's camera interview: "You can be a doctor, lawyer, or whatever it is you want to be. Just make sure that you're the best, and how do you know that you're the best? You gotta eat, sleep, and breath the business so much that it becomes your DNA!" When I first heard these words, they hit me like a hammer on a nail. It just made perfect sense.

 You ever see a horse and buggy, and the horses have these blinders on either side of their heads? Those blinders are there to help them avoid distractions and look straight ahead. I want you to put on your blinders and ignore what these people are saying—all of that negative junk about you anyway—and just keep pushing forward.

 I saw this video clip on YouTube, with Dr. Oz and Tony Robbins, on handling negativity. Here's what I want you to do the next time you are feeling down, depressed, or even anxious. I want you to stand up and place your feet shoulder-width apart. Now place your hands on your hips. This is called the "Superhero Pose." Once you do this, I want you to close your eyes and breath in through your nose and out of your mouth. Do this for two minutes. While doing this, think to yourself that you are more than enough and what others are saying about you is nothing but noise.

How do you become the best in what you do? I'm sure that your company has specific tasks and procedures that you can do daily. This whole process of learning again and again until you get it right is called Repetition Learning. Now, I will be the first to tell you that you will suck at it when you get started, and it will make you feel like you don't know what you're doing. Congratulations, you just passed your first hurdle to getting it done and escalating yourself to the top. Now, I did say that you are going to suck at it. However, the more you do it, the better you're going to be, which will bring you more confidence. The next thing you know, you are an expert, whether in inviting people, doing presentations, or training your staff on carrying out those tasks.

The bottom line is for you to find out what kind of training or tasks your company has in store for you. Then, you got to practice, practice, over and over, and over again, until it becomes second nature. Next, go and train your staff and crew on how to get it done. And don't be afraid to correct them if you see them making any mistakes.

If you are feeling anything but confident, do the Superhero Pose, which goes like this:

1. Take your feet shoulder-width apart
2. Hands on your hips, close your eyes
3. Breathe into your nose and out through your mouth

This exercise should take two minutes. I recommend doing some pushups along with this. Now, they don't have to be perfect; but the more you do it, the better you will get at them. When it comes to people and what they have to say, just put on your blinders and don't let it affect you.

Developing a winning attitude fortifies your success. Most importantly, JUST KEEP PUSHING!!!

## BIOGRAPHY

Denver Duncan has spent twenty years learning and training with the Army and transferring his knowledge from the battlefield to the boardroom. Now, he wants to bring out the best version of you by showing what happens when you take action instead of hesitating and procrastinating.

Contact Denver Duncan via https://linktr.ee/denverduncan

CHAPTER 10

# No U-Turns, Gps, And Foot Checks

*By Donna Shupe*

When I learned to drive at sixteen, there was no such thing as a GPS. You had to know where you were going and watch for signs and exits.

It was very important to watch for the signs that said, "No U-turn." You couldn't go back. You had to go ahead. You could get into serious trouble for making a U-turn when it wasn't allowed, and no one wanted that!

I took part in a workshop a few years later, where everyone was asked to choose the street sign with which they most identified. Without hesitation, I chose "No U-turn." It made sense to me. Keep going forward. Don't go back; plan for the direction you want to go, and go there. Going backward or making a U-turn will not help you achieve your goals. Going backward will slow everything down and prolong the trip. Look forward, go forward. Don't look back, and don't go backward.

For years, this was my philosophy. Things changed. Sometimes, I felt that I was avoiding U-turns and not going forward. I was either stuck in one place or going around and around the same block, not getting anywhere.

My street sign changed over the years. For a while, it was the "Children Crossing" sign. Sometimes, it was "Bumpy Road Ahead." Many times, the sign would have said, "Slow Down." I think I missed a few that warned me of the "Sharp Curves Ahead." I discovered the sign "Limited Visibility" was very accurate. I never knew what lay ahead, either on the road or in my life. I didn't drive off any bridges or cliffs, and it was always a good reminder to "Drive Safe."

I like signs. They help me follow the rules and keep me safe. They tell me how fast I can go and what direction I am going. But do signs limit us? When there is a speed limit, what if you could go faster? Am I accepting limitations that someone else puts on my dreams and goals? Are you?

Who makes the signs that I follow? I decided it was time to make my own signs, to reach for goals by going directions I have not yet ventured—a new and different path. It might not be straight, and I am sure it will be laden with curves and unknown challenges, but I know the journey will be a joyous one—if I let it.

No U-turns. Really? Why not? What if I need to go in a different direction? Does a U-turn always mean going backward?

As I grew older and took many different paths, I also embraced the technological changes that entered my life. No longer did I have to try to re-fold that map (it never folded back the way it originally came anyway!), but I could now follow the directions on a GPS. And that opened the door for a completely different viewpoint on signs, life, and where to go.

GPS stands for Global Positioning System. That means a GPS can pinpoint where you are at any time. Wouldn't it be nice to look at your life and see exactly where you are, how far your destination is, and how to get there? What if you knew that the challenges you are currently facing are 2.7 miles down the road from becoming only a memory? Maybe it would be helpful to know that your anticipated destination is fourteen hours away? Unless you stop for breaks every few miles!

Moving to the GPS from a traditional map or atlas system is different because it doesn't show you the total destination. You are only shown the next turn, and after you have made that one, only then do you see the next one. Although you know your final destination's location, the GPS does not give you the big picture of how to get there. When using a traditional map or atlas, you can look at each step on the journey, plan where you want to stop or detour, and study the details of the final goal.

Sometimes, the GPS does not always get you where you want to go. At one point, I was driving through a place I wasn't familiar with, and I relied on the GPS to get me where I wanted to go. From where I was, I could see the major road that I wanted. But, the GPS sent me one block left, then one block right, then one block left, and another block right, and ended up with a zig-zag path to the place I could have reached easily in a more straightforward manner.

I frequently travel with a friend and business partner. Often, we choose to drive across the country rather than fly. We do this is to enjoy time together, make memories, and usually laugh a lot. One of our first trips together was to Nashville, TN. We were attending a training session for our business, and neither of us knew how to get around in Nashville. We used a traditional map to get from Texas to Tennessee. We saw signs for towns on the drive as we went through Prosper, Hope, and Friendly. They seemed like other signs for life!

When we got into Nashville, we switched to GPS to get to our hotel. Driving through new and unknown territory, we depended on the GPS to get where we wanted to go. We had booked reservations at a hotel, one that we specifically picked because of the indoor pool. As we drove through the town, the GPS often didn't give us enough warning about the following turns. The next thing we would hear was the GPS saying in its ever-cheerful tone, 'MAKE THE NEXT LEGAL U-TURN.' So, we would laugh, turn around, and go the other way. We would usually have to follow that with another U-turn to turn around in the right direction. Then, we could coordinate and make the turn that we had missed previously. This happened once, then twice, then again. We lost count of the number of times that GPS kept repeating, 'MAKE THE NEXT LEGAL U-TURN.' It was a lot. Finally, after many wrong turns, missed turns, U-turns, and much laughter, we made it to the destination given on the GPS. What we found when we got there was not even a hotel. It was a business building on the outskirts of Nashville. There were no hotels to be found anywhere around. So, we tried again. We got in the car. I called the hotel we had booked, found out their physical address, and entered it into the GPS. After a few more U-turns, we did get to our destination, only to find out that the indoor pool we wanted was closed for repair and maintenance.

All of this made me think. Once, my thoughts said you should never make a U-turn to reach your destination. Now, I think it sometimes takes plenty of U-turns and detours to reach the ultimate goal you desire. I see many life lessons from the Nashville trip. One of them is that the GPS didn't get us where we wanted to go because we didn't enter the correct information. The address we started with as our goal and destination was flawed. We got where we said we wanted to go, but it wasn't clearly identified as the place we actually wanted to go. The second lesson is that even if something has a plan, like an indoor swimming pool, sometimes, what really manifests is different from the original plan.

In Nashville, we learned that it is sometimes necessary to not only make a U-turn but to make many U-Turns to get where we want to go. During most of the time in the city, we were not where we wanted to be. We had to readjust. The GPS was good for that; it readjusted several times during the trip. Isn't that like life? We think we know where we want to go, but it takes many changes on the pathway and a willingness to look and travel in a different direction to get there.

Traveling with the same friend, we took another business/training trip to Orlando. Leaving Texas with enough snacks (always be prepared) to sugar up an entire town, we headed to Florida. Driving, laughing, singing, celebrating, we crossed the state lines of Louisiana, Mississippi, Alabama, and into Florida. Maybe we were a little tired, a little excited, or just enjoying the trip. When we crossed into Florida, we noticed a sign over the road. In our punchiness, it said, "FOOT CHECK!" So, we burst into laughter and looked down to check, and yes, our feet were still there! On closer examination, the sign actually read "FDOT Check" (Florida Department of Transportation). We still thought it was hilarious, and each time we saw that sign, we laughed and checked our feet.

As funny as that experience was, it was also a good life lesson. First, you need to laugh, even, and especially, at the ordinary everyday parts of life. Second, where are your feet? If you do a "Foot Check" on a daily, weekly, or monthly basis, what do you find? Are they pointing in the right direction? Can you step over obstacles or go around them? Are your feet moving forward or staying in the same place? Are your feet grounded to the things you need and the things that make you feel good? Are you spending time with the people and places that make you happy, connecting to the outdoors, taking time to breathe, and taking care of yourself? Do you have your foundational plans in place? Do your feet feel heavy, hard to move in any direction? Is it an effort just to put one foot in front of another? Or are your feet happily jumping and leaping as you race to your next destination? Are your feet happy and healthy? Can they skip and hop along? Are you taking good care of your feet, so they take you where you want to go?

Every day, there are lessons we can learn from the signs and the things around us. Every day, we should know where we want to go and where we are actually going. Every day, we should celebrate, laugh, hug, and do the best we can do for another person.

What is my street sign today? Once, it was "No U-Turns," without a doubt. I still believe it is important to move forward, and I have learned that moving forward in a straight line is usually not the case. I also learned the importance of enjoying the journey and the people with us. As I write this, my home state of Texas is trying to recover from the effects of COVID-19, a massive snowstorm, and the aftermath of all these events. People have had to do things differently, make changes, and adjust.

So, what is my street sign today? It is a green light. Go. Go forward. Go do something you have been putting off. Go take care of yourself. Go and help a neighbor. Go. Go breathe, relax, and enjoy. Go laugh. Go spend time with friends and family. Go celebrate. Go for your dreams and goals. Go around the block, both literally and figuratively. Remember that when the light is red, it will turn green again soon. Go. Go with a smile on your face and in your heart. Go on a detour. Go fast or go slow. But, Go! Go in the direction of your heart and your joy. Go. Go and be great. Go and be you.

I end with a quote that always speaks to me:

> *"If you want to arrange it, this world you can change it."*[16]
> —Paul O'Neill, Transiberian Orchestra

Go.

## BIOGRAPHY

Donna is passionate about using her gifts to help others and bring out the pieces of everyday life in a way that makes the mundane memorable. With encouragement from her high school English teacher and a BBA in Business and Communication from Stephen F. Austin State University, Donna has used writing and speaking to inform, entertain, and have fun with clients and audiences all across Texas. She has led workshops and presentations for Stephen F. Austin State University, JCPenney Co. Inc, Christus Trinity Mother Frances Health Systems, Greater East Texas Habitat for Humanity, Kilgore High School, and Presbyterian Women's Retreats. After seeing the vision of the network marketing industry, she loves showing others the possibilities and products. But her greatest accomplishment is being Katherine's mom. Donna wants her writing to encourage other women and girls to stand for themselves and follow their dreams.

Contact Donna Shupe via https://linktr.ee/Donnashupe

---

16  LLC. Pegula Sports & Entertainment, "The Official Website of KeyBank Center, Buffalo, NY," KeyBank Center, accessed April 13, 2021, https://www.keybankcenter.com/details/2019-12-14/transsiberian-orchestra-121419330.

CHAPTER 11

# Why I Did Not Give Up When It Was The Easiest Thing To Do

*By Douglas Chee*

It was past midnight, and I was seated alone. My hand held my head up; my eyes were wet, but I could not cry. Maybe I did not want to cry because I was too angry—angry at myself.

For the first time in thirty-three years, I wanted to kill myself. The first time I ever thought of killing myself was when I was fifteen, but that was a lifetime back. This time, it was different; I *wanted* to jump.

I walked to the balcony, and I leaned over, wondering if this was the best place to jump to my death with no chances of survival. I checked three other places, looking for the best spot to jump. I had to make sure that this would end it all and not leave me maimed. 'I must not survive this,' I thought. I could not bear the idea of having people in my life take care of a vegetable.

Several thoughts went through my mind: coward, asshole, taker, irresponsible, you are going to ruin it for your family, friends, and students. It would be the biggest "f@#% you" to everyone that mattered. I couldn't do it. I started to see the faces of my family flashing before me as the tears began to fall.

Then, another thought crossed my mind: would all of my insurance pay out if I committed suicide? I actually didn't know, but would it matter? Of course, it would! All of the money I spent on insurance and financial plans might go to waste! I started to laugh so loud that if anyone had seen me, they would have thought I was losing my mind—maybe I was.

How did I get here? I was tired, lonely, bitter, and angry at myself for allowing myself to get to this point. December 2018, lying in bed after my spine surgery, I promised that I would live life differently if my following medical procedure in April 2019 would go smoothly. I got tired of fighting a losing battle with my business partner. Compromising what I stood for and dealing with her insecurities had been a Sisyphean battle since March 2017. I should have left then.

I did not. I got comfortable—shame on me for betraying myself.

I have trained and coached approximately 50,000 people in the last twenty-four years; I should have known better. I am finally "swallowing my own medicine"—humble pie. So here I was, about to be undone. Did anyone see the person I was—me, my titles, my reputation—and all the roles I played? I never considered it to be a burden, only a privilege. But still. Who am I? What am I? Had I allowed myself to be caged by my success?

I have had a full life. I've gone from "bus class" to business class and back down and up again several times, from working three jobs and walking home. I know what going hungry feels like. I had failed so many times, but I have had my wins. I knew that I did not want to be poor, so I worked hard—very hard.

Mama told me growing up:

'You are a child of mixed parentage; you belong nowhere in the racial divide of Malaysia.'

'You look neither Chinese nor Indian; your skin colour is brown, and you gotta look out for yourself.'

'Don't expect any handouts; you got to do it on your own.'

She also said the following:

'Always do what you are paid to do well. Once you do it well, learn other people's jobs. Don't stop learning.'

'You are both your best friend and worst enemy—do not compare with anyone else.'

Those were my mantras. I hung on to those words, and they carried me through my teenage years. One of my own mantras was 'Don't be poor.' I can't remember how many times I repeated those words and how they drove me. Later in life, I discovered how my own affirmation didn't work as it did not lead me to abundance and prosperity. I was clear then, and even now—money didn't drive me. However, many other things did.

I started working part-time when I was thirteen. I was glad that I looked so much older for my age back then. By the age of twenty-four, I was running a company, a start-up that I had helped grow but did not own. I had reached the top of the organization and felt empty and unfulfilled. Then, my PA and party-buddy inspired me to attend a new life-altering training, which changed everything. After I completed my training, I kissed the corporate world goodbye. I fell in love with personal transformation work, and eventually, I became a master trainer.

I resigned in March 2005 and finally left in May. I made too many compromises in the last two years working for them and exhausted myself. While I had the extra time on my hands, I decided to learn about real estate, insurance, and financial planning and eventually chose to be involved with network marketing while conducting seminars all over Asia. The reason I chose network marketing was because of the nature of relationships I could create. People became partners; they weren't customers or clients, and I enjoyed the personal development side of it.

The fact that I went into network marketing pissed off many people. I didn't care about their judgments and opinions as their opinions would not pay my bills. I read many books by other successful people and knew this company was going to close down. I warned them. They eventually did, six months later.

It was a great learning experience. I learnt what not to do.

Then, I moved on to another program and had the opportunity to travel the world and learn a great deal about MLM. Alas, the company folded, and I decided to go back to a traditional business to do what I love: Transformational Training.

When I started this company, my goal was to replace myself with many trainers and to ensure that succession planning was in place as I did not want to exchange time for money. I wanted to be a real business owner instead of a glorified or delusional business owner who thinks he is one but is still a skilled "employee" exchanging time for money (I'm referring to the cash flow quadrant by Robert Kiyosaki).

We grew a considerably well-sized training business, and in nine years, we exceeded all expectations.

So, there we were in March 2020, another "March" in my life where things were about to change. The first two weeks of a series of lockdowns in Malaysia were about to commence. These were poorly planned by a one-month-old government that got into power through some shenanigans and resulted in me ranting on Facebook on May 17th. I felt it was a forced holiday for the planet. I loved most of the first two weeks of the lockdown. I appreciated the peace and the quiet. For the last nine years, I have lived much of my life in training rooms. It was time for a break. Little did I know, this was simply the calm before the storm.

2020 was planned to be one of my best years. My schedule was packed for the whole year, and I was getting ready to plan 2021. By June of every year, the following year's schedule would already be locked in. That's how I have lived for the last eight years. Somewhat predictable, with time commitments and income. This global pandemic threw a spanner at the works. The whole planet was in the same storm. However, each person was on a different boat. Some were on yachts; some were hanging for their life on a dinghy; some had only a lifejacket. We went from living a somewhat predictable life to living one day at a time.

After two weeks of a "forced pause," I took the opportunity to catch up on reading, binge-watching TV and YouTube, attend online seminars to learn (also to see what other people were doing), and deal with the fortnightly headache of rescheduling our seminars. The light at the end of this tunnel was an on-coming train!

The work we did was face-to-face, active, passionate, raw, and intense. It was special, and for most, life-defining moments were created.

We decided to bring the shutters down permanently. Here's why:

1. To move it all online felt like a giant sell-out. We started to morph some of the training sessions as best we could, and about half of our graduates supported it—the other half didn't.
2. The company could not sustain the monthly expenses to keep itself going, and we had twenty people on staff. We would have consumed what we had in the bank within six months.
3. The request for refunds, including all those that were not eligible, started pouring in.
4. Inefficient government policies and going in and out of lockdowns made planning impossible.

I did not grieve. I did not have the space to do so. It was my baby dying too.

Over the last three years, I had sold out my purpose on why I started this company in the first place. I tolerated my partner's insecurities and allowed the success of the business to dictate the quality of the trainings. It became unrecognizable in terms of what I stood for. I eroded my own principles, tolerated, and made too many compromises.

It takes two hands clapping to make a sound, but I will take responsibility for my actions.

As decided, I numbed myself from experience and decided to charge ahead and plan my next steps. I didn't show any compassion for those grieving over the closure of this wonderful platform we created.

I was thankful that my gold and silver trading portfolios were doing well. That, however, was not going to give me the cash flow I needed. I was asset-rich but cash-flow poor. So, I decided to go back into network marketing. Many people were going to be in a similar position, and many vilified me for that choice.

Life is too precious to live by other people's expectations. I needed to spend time with people who would celebrate me versus tolerate me, surround myself with people I would celebrate, not tolerate. I learned that it's okay not to be okay sometimes, that I am nothing but what I create. I needed to practice forgiving myself because I allowed myself to be manipulated and controlled by people who did not deserve that power over me.

I still have much to contribute, and my contribution matters.

I will create my own tribe, focusing on manifesting wealth and prosperity by generating multiple streams of income, not just through network marketing. We have to pandemic-proof our income.

I will continue with my passion and build a new training platform, and this time, anchoring quality over quantity and staying true without compromising my integrity, with the end in mind.

On the last day of all my seminars, I tell all the participants that I am a "work in progress"—that I am not done. Who I am becoming is more important than who I was. I will never be done, and that is okay. If I can go to bed knowing I made a small difference today and that I was a better man today than I was yesterday, that is enough.

> *"The wheel turns, the struggle continues,*
> *and the command is always the same. Be True. Stand."*[17]
> *—Mother Abigail, The Stand by Stephen King*

---

[17] Matthew Jackson, "With His New Ending for The Stand, Stephen King Answers One of His Fiction's Oldest Questions," SYFY WIRE (SYFY WIRE, February 12, 2021), https://www.syfy.com/syfywire/the-stand-new-ending-stephen-king-coda.

## BIOGRAPHY

Douglas Chee is a Transformational Trainer specializing in Experiential Education for the personal transformational movement. He has trained in Hong Kong, Taipei, China, Singapore, Indonesia, and Malaysia. Douglas played a vital and pivotal role in writing, developing, and training the Character Building Module of the Malaysian National Service Programme for the Government of Malaysia, which included the design and delivery of the Training of Trainers component. He has trained and coached over 50,000 people in leadership, breakthrough, awareness, intimacy, sexuality, mastery, abundance and prosperity, communications, and relationships throughout Asia for over twenty-five years. He owned and ran a successful training company. Douglas has an MBA. He enjoys reading non-fiction and spending time with his family. He was also a certified stuntman. He is now an aspiring author and entrepreneur, and he supports others to create wealth, abundance, and prosperity.

Contact Douglas Chee via https://linktr.ee/douglasalexchee

CHAPTER 12

# New Beginnings

*By Elizabeth McCoon*

Imagine sitting in your car on a November night, after dropping one kid off at her daycare provider's home and one kid off with his father because they needed a warm place to stay. You begin to wonder if this is it. Is this how your life is going to be? You cry because you were kicked out of where you lived, with two toddlers, and begin to wonder if this life is even worth living. Imagine sitting in the cold car because you are almost out of gas, no clue where to go next or who to ask for help, and not having the slightest idea of what tomorrow will bring. All this really puts life into perspective for you.

    I sat in my car, tired, stressed, hungry, and unsure of my future. I was only sure of my kids' safety, even if it was just for the night. In that car, I began to contemplate suicide. I began to consider signing my children's rights over to their father. I began to question my choices in life. I began to wonder if I was going to be okay. I began . . .

    Life is a set of new beginnings, and I once had dreams of who I wanted to become as an adult. I had dreams of becoming a millionaire. I dreamed of the perfect beginning and the perfect ending. Life would have been easy. I have had many starts in my life; none of them were perfect, but all of them have brought me to the place I am now, and all of them have made me who I am today.

    It was in that car that I began to recall all my beginnings. I am a child of divorced parents. I am a child of an absentee father who was emotionally abusive. I am a child of a single mother who did her best. I am a child who never felt her self-worth. I am a child who was repeatedly knocked down in life. I am a child that couldn't dream. I am a child who contemplated suicide. I am a child of self-harm and self-defeat. I am a child.

One of the major new beginnings in my life was letting go of my biological father. My parents divorced when I was young. I do not remember much of them being together, but I know they were far better apart than together. They fought endlessly, and often my sister and I suffered because of it. There were times it would get so bad that my sister swore to me that she would take me away and protect me when she turned eighteen. My father became very emotionally abusive. Our visits with him would feel more like an interrogation. He would ask way too many questions about our mom and her boyfriend, and occasionally he would ask about school. Eventually, our visits to him would stop. We would find other things to do during the summers instead of going there. The abuse never stopped. All the phone calls that we had were always about how I would never make anything of myself and always live in poverty with my mother. He would call us white trash. He made me feel worthless and unloved. I was thirteen when I finally had to face the hard truth. My father was gone. He became nothing more than a mere figure in my rear-view mirror. I wanted to forget him; I wanted to not love him. But I could not. I tried, and tried, to have a relationship with him until the fateful day I first contemplated suicide because of him.

Although it may sound a little silly, this was the biggest accomplishment of my life at the time. I was graduating from the eighth grade. I prepared for the day, pretending as if everything was fine, but I was dying inside. My dad knew the day; I made sure of it on the last phone call. Why did he forget? Why did he not call to celebrate with me? He used to tell me how much he missed me. Did he really? Was he not proud of me? How could he not be? Although the graduation was amazing, and my mom's side of the family was there to celebrate this occasion, there was one person from whom I wanted support; but he never did. I felt like my heart had been ripped out of my chest. What was the point of going on? All I wanted was for both of my parents to love me and be proud of me, but he didn't. I thought that if I were no longer on this earth, then maybe he would love me. Maybe he would feel sad. Maybe he would miss me. I knew that I couldn't give up. I knew, even at such a young age, that I could not give up and that I had a greater purpose. I knew that I needed a new beginning.

I have always had a "never give up" attitude. I may have temporarily lost it along the way sometimes, but when I became a mom, I realized that giving up was never an option. When I had to lie to my children that I would eat later, knowing that there was not enough food for the three of us, I became hungrier, not for food but a better future. When food stamps ran out, and when I faced eviction with two toddlers, I desired to find a fresh start. There was no other option. I could not accept defeat or failure. I simply hit the grind harder just to show my children that being at the bottom gave me the strength I needed to live the life we deserved.

I know now that having children at a young age has been a blessing for me. It kept me from making choices that were selfish and potentially life-ruining. I was forced to think about my children's safety and well-being constantly. Being a young mom has had its own set of difficulties—ones that I faced throughout my life. I thought I was prepared for them, having been raised by a single mom, but that definitely was not the case. I dealt with the struggles of balancing work, school, and raising children. People always told me I should have waited to have children until I was ready. Is anyone ever really ready for parenthood or the struggles that come with it? I wasn't prepared to get evicted. I wasn't prepared to see my five-year-old son suffer a stroke. I wasn't prepared to live on welfare. I wasn't prepared to raise a child with disabilities. I wasn't prepared.

I can recall sitting in the PICU, looking at my son hooked up to all the machines, struggling to speak, tears falling from his eyes, and feeling so helpless. I hated seeing him like this. He was such an active five-year-old. He was wise beyond his years. Looking at him so helplessly lying there was the most heart-breaking thing. He didn't understand what was happening. There were nights when I refused to leave his side. I had already left him once when they took him by helicopter to the hospital, and I was unsure if he would live. During the initial hospital stay, the one thing that I remember most was him saying, "Mom, I wish I would just die." When I asked him why he said that, he replied that he didn't want me to cry anymore. That tore me apart. I was the parent. I needed to be his strength; I needed to show him there was always a better way. It was right there that I made a vow to myself: I needed to show him he was meant for a greater purpose as I knew I was when I was younger. I needed to be his support, his cheering squad. I knew that I needed to push him to become his best self; in return, I would force myself to be better. I had to help him with his new beginning. He needed me now more than ever. There was nothing more powerful than propelling my dreams and finding my success because of my kids.

I wanted to become a role model to them. I wanted to show them that it's not about where you started but rather where you end up. I needed to show my kids that with hard work and a dream, we could find the better life we deserved. I would constantly imagine being gone and seeing my kids live a life of total unfulfillment. They would never find that one thing that made them happy. They would settle for a career, not a passion. They would settle for a marriage, not true love. They would feel defeat and despair. I despised the feeling that I would leave this world behind and not have made a difference in their lives. I would have taught my children to settle.

I began to look for that better future. I started to dream again. I started by pursuing a degree. I started by advancing into a management position at the age of nineteen. I started to focus on personal financial goals. I started to give my kids the best life I possibly could. I worked and went to school, both full-time, and still, I was drowning. We had a cute little apartment, but I was struggling to pay all the bills alone. I needed to start looking for other sources of income. I needed to start looking for my kid's financial future and security. I needed to start a new beginning.

I tried many things that had the promise of success, and I failed. I invested time and money only to get nowhere. People thought I was crazy. People said I could never become a millionaire with these types of side jobs. I began to believe that I was destined to struggle for my entire life. I was ready to settle for an unfulfilling career where I would never get ahead. I began to see my dream of becoming a millionaire slowly fade away. I was unable to figure out why I kept failing. What was I missing? What was it that made others succeed but not me? Passion. Passion was the one thing that I lacked. Passion for what I was striving for, passion for success, passion in myself. It was the thing holding me back. It took me years and two failed marriages to realize where my passion was. I had to find something that ignited a fire so deep in my soul that it could not be ignored. Passion is not enough; it's more than that. I needed to not do it alone. I needed to find a group of people that had the same passion. I needed to find a support system that would be my cornerstone. I needed to find the people who would cheer me on, celebrate all my milestones, and lift me up during my failures. I needed to find my support system!

In these moments of "failure," I found my self-worth. I found my true passion and my true calling. I found my support system. I found my cheering squad. I found people who would encourage me to be better. I found my new beginning. I have left all the negativity behind so that I can give my family the future they deserve.

I found my new beginning.

## BIOGRAPHY

Liz McCoon is considered many things. She is an entrepreneur, a mother, a daughter, and a friend. She is strong and loyal. Her strength and loyalty are rooted in her belief in treating others as you want to be treated. She is a beautiful, caring person who is motivated to pursue her dreams. She has the attitude that she can do all things. Liz has pushed her boundaries and has excelled in all that she has strived for. She continues to be committed to showing others that if she can accomplish greatness, then so can they.

Contact Elizabeth McCoon via https://linktr.ee/Lizmccoon21

CHAPTER 13

# Pain As A Catalyst

*By Eric Ranks*

You know the phrase, "It's not what happens to you in life but how you react to it?" I have experienced several moments that have mentally and physically knocked me down. Suddenly losing my father in 2019 was one of the hardest experiences I've ever gone through. What I wouldn't give for one more game night with him, to watch his eyes light up when he won, or hear his boisterous laugh. However, many other moments made me ponder this phrase over and over again: my various health struggles; and the times I failed in school and my business. However, I never let these failures hold me back.

My journey began in November 1984 at the age of six. My father was in the Air Force. We were stationed at Loring AFB in Limestone, Maine. During this time, I became extremely sick. The doctors at the military hospital ran tests. My white blood cell count, one of the many tests, came back extremely high. This, and other tests, determined that I had Leukemia. I needed to be medevaced to Bethesda Naval Hospital in Bethesda, Maryland (currently Walter Reed National Military Medical Center) for further testing and treatment. Fun fact: they also found out that my kidneys were connected as one, resembling a horseshoe. Prior to being flown to Bethesda, I had a blessing of healing from my local church members. After that blessing, I started to feel better and my lab results showed that my Leukemia was no longer traceable. I believe that I was cured of Leukemia through the power of prayer, faith, and Divine intervention. How else can a recovery like this be explained? This sparked my lifelong belief that I had a higher calling and led me to ask myself, 'What's my purpose?'

As a young man who beat Leukemia, I felt invincible. I was in shape, ran around town with friends all hours of the night, and never once thought it would end—until it almost did. At the age of 18, I cheated death after being involved in a major car accident; my survival surprised many. At the hospital, a police officer brought me the steering wheel, which I ripped off the steering column as a result of my adrenaline rush during the accident.

Later, I went through a divorce that put me through some very dark times. I gained a lot of weight due to the depression, and almost OD'd on antidepressants (which I took to try and bring back the happiness I felt I had lost). On this night, Divine intervention saved my life once again. I had the urge to call 911 because I knew something was wrong. After all that, I thought I was done facing death. After turning 35, I had an eventful six years during which I constantly reminded myself that I was here for a reason.

During the summer of 2014, I noticed something was very wrong. My wife and I were at my sister's lake house in Idaho relaxing over the 4$^{th}$ of July break. We decided to take a paddleboat out to explore the lake. Ten minutes into our trip, I told her we had to go back. I had suddenly felt fatigued and lost energy. I was worried that I wouldn't be able to help get us back to shore. Once back at the house, I decided to take a nap. I slept most of the day but still felt tired and weak throughout the evening. We decided to head home early the next day and made the drive back to our home in Utah. When we got home that afternoon, I decided to get checked out at our local clinic to try and figure out what was going on. After a quick checkup, the doctor told me that I had some sort of internal bleeding, and he encouraged me to take some medication for ulcers.

The next morning, I spoke to my dad about my symptoms and the doctor's recommendations. My dad said he had a strong urge to call our family doctor and get her opinion. She advised that I go to the Emergency

Room immediately. Once I arrived, the doctors and nurses ran my lab results and confirmed that I was extremely anemic. They gave me my first of two blood transfusions and began other tests to determine what was going on. Ten days later, after multiple Endoscopies and Colonoscopies, I was diagnosed with Arteriovenous malformations (AVMs). These are an abnormal tangle of arteries and veins that can weaken and rupture. They believed an autoimmune disease likely caused this but were unable to pinpoint which one. They cauterized the AVMs as they found them, but I kept showing signs of internal bleeding. Due to this, I couldn't leave the hospital. It was a 'wait and see' game at this point.

A couple of days later, I was finally allowed to eat solid food; that's when things went from bad to worse. The doctor called to check on me and heard my machines going crazy in the background. She ran upstairs and saw that I was extremely tachycardic, so she decided to perform an emergency procedure to find out what was happening. As many might know, eating food right before surgery is not ideal, so this procedure had to take place in the ICU. It was during that procedure that I aspirated, which in turn caused my stomach to herniate through my diaphragm. Without being in the ICU, I would not likely have survived.

After three weeks, my internal bleeding was under control, and I was healthy enough to go home with a surgery scheduled to fix my hernia. Over the next year, internal bleeding was a non-issue, although I was warned that it would happen again due to the number of AVMs I had. Not wanting to go through that experience again, I began researching preventative measures. It was during this research that I found out about the Ketogenic diet and how many diseases and illnesses were tied to metabolic syndrome. I had never heard of this before. Having Type II diabetes and being diagnosed with Non-Alcoholic Steatohepatitis (NASH) at the time, I was intrigued. This ultimately started my journey with the Ketogenic diet. I read everything I could find on the subject and started a Facebook group for those wanting to learn about the Ketogenic diet and the medical studies tied to it. Through this group, I also started networking with leaders in the Ketogenic community and building lifelong friendships.

This lifestyle played a major role in my next four years. I witnessed the impacts of proper nutrition as my Type II diabetes and NASH were reversed, my internal bleeding stayed at bay, and I lost over 100 lbs. I was proud of my accomplishment in my health journey. Being a part of the Ketogenic community sparked my passion for health coaching and helping others on their wellness journey. I had found my purpose! I was inspired to help people find the root cause of their health issues instead of focusing on only weight loss and dieting. Without having gone through the hell I experienced, I would not have found my passion for health and nutrition.

As the years went on, I strayed from Keto and fell back into some old habits tied to fast food and poor nutrition. This would turn out to be my undoing and bring me to my next fight with death. In the summer of 2019, I started having pains in my stomach and other issues that were very persistent. After working with a gastroenterologist, it was determined that I had a blockage in my stomach. To make things worse, my hernia from years ago was creeping back up. However, it didn't seem severe enough to receive much attention, so we focused more on my stomach blockage. But four months later, that little hernia would cause a major issue. It rubbed up against my esophagus and caused a perforation that was quite deadly. I was told that less than 50% of people survive this. After an emergency procedure, my family and I thanked the surgeon for saving my life. He stated that it was some sort of Divine intervention that saved me and that he didn't do it on his own. My case was something he had only seen once or twice in 18 years. While I genuinely believe that a higher power was present in that room during the surgery, I also believe that my father, who had passed away a few months before, was by my side.

These are just some of the experiences that prove to me that I have a higher purpose. Whenever I hit rock bottom, I reflect on the fear and pain I felt during those times and remember that I need to pull myself up and strive to be the best I can be. For me, this is my 'Why.' While getting back to optimal health is an ongoing process, I don't lose sight of my purpose in helping others with their own journey. Helping and motivating other people has always been important to me. When I've created businesses or advanced my own life skills, I ask the question: How can what I have or know help others? I would like to help them as I did myself, turning the focus of my own health journey into being a Certified Health Coach, in order to teach them the importance of nutrition and the human body.

Another way I used my 'Why' to help others is by co-founding a non-profit 501(c)(3) called "The Veterans Connection" (TVC) in 2012. TVC is dedicated to enhancing the quality of life for individual veterans and their families. Our mission is to assure every Veteran who served and protected our country is provided resources for mental health, PTSD, and suicide prevention. The Veterans Connection was created with the vision to assure that every veteran is provided for in the manner befitting those who have protected and served our great country.

I've gone through many rough patches in my life. Through it all, not only do I have my 'Why' at the forefront of my actions, but also some principles that help me get through the dark times and drive success. I'd like to share them with you, along with some of my favorite quotes.

> *"The value we provide most to others is the same value we appreciate most from others."*—Simon Sinek

Live your life centered around building relationships. Whether it's personal or professional, always look for opportunities to provide value without asking for anything in return. This will then allow you to ask for help when you need it because you've given them more value than what you're asking for.

> *"Find your Why and you'll find your Way."*—John C. Maxwell

Always remember your 'Why.' Mine would cross my mind every time I remembered that I've been saved on multiple occasions for a higher purpose. This is my 'Why,' and using that belief has helped me pick myself up and keep moving forward.

*"Learn how to be happy with what you have while you pursue all that you want."*—Jim Rohn

Focus on daily gratitude. This is an extremely powerful exercise in changing your mindset from negative to positive. Every morning I write down two things for which I'm grateful and read a motivational quote. This then sets a positive tone for the day.

*"Be here now."*—Dr. Ryan Lowery

How powerful would the relationships around you be if you were always in the present? No distractions like phones, talking to someone else, or thinking about your to-do list for tomorrow. Be mindful, be present.

*"There are no secrets to success. It is the result of preparation, hard work, and learning from failure."*—Colin Powell

Outworking other people will always bring in higher returns than those who may be more skilled around you. When starting a new job or creating my non-profit, I didn't know what to do or how to do it. However, that didn't stop me from working harder than the others to be the best.

*"Diligent follow-up and follow-through will set you apart from the crowd and communicate excellence."*—John C. Maxwell

Years ago, a friend taught me: "The fortune is in the follow-up." This principle has greatly enhanced my personal and sales career, allowing me to succeed where others have failed.

*"Make Positivity Louder."*—Gary Vaynerchuk

For those reading this book, I ask that we join together in drowning out the negative noise around us and instead fill the world with positivity. There is strength in numbers, and if we shift our mindset together, we can become who we want to be and influence those around us.

Lastly, I want to leave you with this:

*"You have power over your mind, not outside events. Realize this, and you will find strength."* —Marcus Aurelius

If you're going through struggles, know that you're still here because you have a purpose. I know it can be hard to understand that while going through the dark times, but finding your 'Why' through the struggles and sharing your experiences may one day motivate others to find their own purpose.

## BIOGRAPHY

Eric Ranks is an author, self-made entrepreneur, motivational speaker, corporate executive with over 24 years experience in sales training and leadership, and seven years in digital marketing working with some of the world's largest digital marketing companies. In 2012 he established a non-profit organization, 'The Veterans Connection,' where he serves as President and Executive Director. Eric is also a Certified Health and Keto Coach, and his entrepreneurial spirit inspired him to create GATA Travel in 2000. Eric's journey hasn't been an easy one. Deadly health challenges almost robbed Eric of his life, and what's worse, the pursuit of his dreams. Eric's first book, *Boundless Success*, includes his story about overcoming multiple near-death experiences and finding his "why," his reason to fight and live. Eric has a passion for helping people and inspires others to never give up, helps them overcome life's challenges, and guides them on a fast path to realizing the value already in them.

Dream Bigger, Live Better!

Connect with Eric Ranks via https://bio.ericranks.club

CHAPTER 14

# Walking Down The Road With A Gas Can

*By Greg Theobald*

I woke up on a beautiful Saturday morning in June. It was the end of my working week on graveyard patrol. I loved being a street cop, and I also loved the weekend. But this morning, something was different. I could sense it, but I couldn't place my finger on it. I went downstairs and looked around. The computer, TV, and several other items were missing. I walked over to the kitchen table and found a small post-it note. The note was from my then wife. It read something like this: *I need to be by myself now. I'll be house-sitting for a while. Don't try to find me, because you are not allowed here. The guard at the gate has your name and knows you are not welcome here.*

I ran upstairs and looked in our bathroom and closet; everything was gone. My head was spinning. After thirty-five years of marriage and four children, all I got to show for it was a post-it note saying goodbye. I had long suspected that day might come, but still, I was not ready for it. Even after being ridiculed, scolded, verbally and physically threatened, and abused, I was still afraid to lose the relationship.

We had been going to counseling for several months prior to her leaving. After we had been subjected to long hours of questions from the Diagnostic and Statistical Manual on mental Illness, the counselor finally diagnosed my wife as suffering from Borderline Personality Disorder (or BPD), a severe mental illness. She had developed BPD due to the trauma she had suffered as an adolescent at the hands of her parents. Her father had sexually molested her, and when her mother found out about it, she had done nothing to protect her child.

When the counselor told me my wife had a severe mental illness, bells and whistles went off in my mind. Suddenly, her behavior over the last three decades made sense. My mind reeled from the blow. Through my job, I had been trained in crisis intervention for the mentally ill. I had served dozens of commitment orders and transported dozens of mentally ill people to where they would receive the right sort of help. I had received many hours of training on dealing with mentally ill subjects. So, why hadn't I seen what had been happening right in front of me for so long?

The counselor said, "You are the victim of a loveless marriage." He continued, "She doesn't love you; she has never loved you, and she can't love you in the future." He further told me he had never seen such a long relationship with a person suffering from BPD. The counselor figured our marriage had survived for so long because I was so accustomed to taking abuse in my job that I had accepted it at home, as well.

To understand how the situation had come about, you first need to know where I came from. I grew up in Southern California with my mom and my stepdad, who had joined our family when I was two years old. My parents had divorced just before I was born, and I used to visit my dad every other weekend and during the summers.

As a young child in grade school, I'd had to wear special shoes with braces on them, like Forrest Gump's, because I was extremely pigeon-toed, and I would trip myself up when I walked. Because we couldn't afford the special shoes, I had to wear my shoes on the wrong feet to help train them to point in the right direction. I was ridiculed and shamed relentlessly. I had sworn to those who made fun of me that I would one day run faster and longer than anyone on the planet. But that had only created more ridicule and teasing. I grew up feeling very angry, yet I was also determined.

I had always felt as though I didn't have a real home, and I had covered up that feeling by playing the comedian. By the time I reached high school, I had become the class clown, the life of the party. I began my running career in high school, on the cross-country and track teams. I loved running, and I was relentless and very good at it.

In my youth, I had developed a strong desire to make the world a better place. One day, while riding in my friend's car, I saw two men trying to steal another man's bike from him. I told my friend to stop the car. I immediately got out, ran toward the two men while screaming and yelling at the top of my lungs. I must have startled them enough to make them put down the bike and run because that's precisely what they did. I checked on the man who owned the bike to ensure he was okay and ran back to the car. My friend was in complete shock and told me I was crazy. Somehow, though, I felt a deep sense of satisfaction at having done the right thing and helped someone in need.

As my teenage years rolled by, I had always feared I would never have a real family. I wanted a family where both parents stayed married, and the children grew up to honor their parents. I wanted to create a legacy of family togetherness. I acted out of this fear at age fifteen and latched on to a girl, although she always treated me badly. I ignored her bad behavior because she was aesthetically pleasing to me. I took her pushing me away as a challenge, and I was determined to win her love. Four years later, my dedication and persistence paid off. She was mine at seventeen, and we married as high school sweethearts at nineteen.

I woke up the morning after our honeymoon with a sick feeling in my stomach. I had failed to listen to my friends' and my mother's advice not to marry her. But I had pushed my feelings aside and told myself that it was normal. Many of us act out of fear and need, which makes us do things we feel comfortable with, even if the results turn out to be poor or devastating.

My stepdad and grandpa were law officers, and I wanted to follow suit. I told my then wife I was going to be a police officer. When I wasn't hired immediately, she ridiculed me and told me to give up and try something else. Her attitude only made me more determined to reach my goal. I'll show her, I thought; then she'll be proud of me. I persisted with sheer grit and determination, and I was finally hired as a police officer.

To this day, I still don't feel she was ever proud of me. It seems that, sometimes, we do the right things for the wrong reasons and for the wrong person.

My reasons for becoming a police officer were deeply rooted in my desire to serve and help others. Besides that, I did not want to die an unknown man. I wanted my life to mean something, to have significance. I knew if I were killed in the line of duty, I would have the American flag draped over my coffin, hundreds of fellow officers and civilians would attend my funeral, and I would be memorialized as a hero forever. I would have my name on the wall at the National Law Enforcement Memorial. I got great satisfaction from knowing that.

I loved the life of a street cop, even though it meant responding to one traumatic event after another. But after thirty years on the street, the emotions I had pushed down deep inside me for so long inevitably started to come to the surface. I knew they were changing me, and I felt them coming on with a vengeance. Often, we try to keep our feelings locked up inside, even though we know it only hurts us in the long run. We sometimes do it out of fear—fear of being ridiculed, fear of the unknown, fear of not being loved. There's a quote from the movie *After Earth*, in which Will Smith's character says something about fear that rings true to me: "Fear is not real. The only place that fear can exist is in our thoughts of the future. It is the product of our imagination, causing us to fear things that do not at present and may not ever exist. That is near insanity. Now, do not misunderstand me, danger is very real, but fear is a choice."

My two best friends, with whom I had worked for eighteen years, could see the difference in me and that it was affecting my performance and safety. To make matters worse, that was when my then wife left me because I was now eligible for retirement. I discovered she had filed for divorce even before we had picked out a property together for our retirement home and before she had convinced me to buy her a new car. She had only stayed with me to get half my pension. Of course, I became a complete mess, and I felt very lost. I had always planned on retiring in August 2017, but when the day finally came and went, my two buddies sat me down and told me it was time for me to retire. They told me that I was lucky to still be alive and physically healthy after having worked the streets for thirty years. To stay any longer would be tempting fate.

My friends loved me enough to tell me the truth and help me see the reality of the situation. Once I had realized they were right, I put in my retirement letter, and I finally retired in September 2017.

Once retired, I sought counseling and coaching and started allowing myself to have and express feelings, the feelings I had pushed down as a police officer. I also had to realize I am the one who teaches others how to treat me. I was responsible for the thirty-five years of abuse I had suffered. I had allowed fear to rule my decision-making. I had been taking care of others at the expense of losing myself. No longer working as a police officer, I had now lost my platform to help others. It felt as though my tank had run dry, and I was now walking on the side of the road with a gas can. I knew I had to reinvent myself, to get back to being the person who had always loved and served others.

I took responsibility for my horrendous mistakes. I also forgave myself for making them. I sought help from counselors and mentors, and with hard work and persistence, I have emerged as a better person. It hasn't been easy, but now I know how to keep my tank full, so I can continue to help others.

I also realized that my strong desire to serve and protect others came out of a deep love for my fellow beings. When I look back on the people I have helped and served over the years, I realized I felt real love for many of them. I'm now practicing what I have learned about love from Dr. Greg Baer: "Real Love is caring about the happiness of another person without any thought for what we might get for ourselves. When we give Real Love, we're not disappointed, hurt, or angry, even when people are thoughtless, or inconsiderate, or give us nothing in return—including gratitude—because our concern is for their happiness, not our own. Real Love is unconditional."

Giving real love can be very hard, and it takes practice. Today, I'm happier than I've ever been because I know I was put on earth to love and serve others and help them achieve better lives, full of meaning and significance. I truly believe these words from Napoleon Hill: "Whatever the mind of man can conceive and believe, it can achieve."

I still have days when the emotional trauma from the past surfaces and makes me cry, but now I know it's okay to show my emotions. I no longer push my feelings down and try to act tough because sharing emotions is the only way to truly have a meaningful relationship with others. Without meaningful relationships, life is not worth living. Sure, we take risks when we are vulnerable, but as I have learned from Dr. Baer, "True happiness is our entire reason to live, and that kind of happiness can only be obtained as we find real love and share it with others. With real love, nothing else matters; without it, nothing else is enough."

## BIOGRAPHY

Greg Theobald served and protected people for thirty years as a dedicated street cop. Greg earned his counseling degree on the streets through trial by fire. Seeing the grief, pain, hopelessness, and suffering in the world tugged at his heart, inspiring him to make a real difference in people's lives. Greg went above and beyond the call of duty, taking time to counsel people to help them improve their lives. Greg's caring dedication to serve others has not ceased but grown. With his years of acquired knowledge, expert insights, and street wisdom, Greg is still inspiring and helping people live happy and meaningful lives full of love.

Contact Greg Theobald via https://linktr.ee/Greg.Theobald

CHAPTER 15

# Your New Diagnosis: Pain-Free

*By Guillermo De Novi*

"AGH!" I yelled as I felt what could have been a knife jam into my lower-right back. I collapsed to the ground and crashed onto my knees as tears rushed to my eyes. I had never experienced such searing pain, and I was only fifteen years old.

I was so close to the finish line of my 200-meter sprint. It was supposed to be the final run of an ordinary practice during freshman year of high school. But that moment proved to be the catalyst that led to my dream of changing the world by helping people eliminate unnecessary pain and return to a life full of joy and freedom.

It's a beautiful gift that most of us are born with a healthy body, a calm, present mind, and a playful soul.

And then, LIFE happens.

We endure a devastating physical injury, emotional trauma, or have our dreams crushed. Having any one of these can create a disconnect between our body, mind, and spirit. The result is chronic pain.

This pain can be acknowledged, dealt with, released, and can become a growth experience.

This pain can also be ignored by strengthening our ego, managed through pharmacology. It can be suppressed into our subconscious and transformed into neuromuscular tension that takes the form of physical pain and symptoms for the rest of our lives.

Chronic pain is always present in the background. From the moment we wake up, it greets us. Throughout the day, it exists in the form of white noise, affecting the way we think and feel, destroying our ability to connect to our loved ones, preventing us from feeling true joy and excitement. But like clockwork, at the end of our day, it kisses us goodnight and occasionally zaps us awake to make sure we don't forget about it.

I was there. For eight long years.

There are countless stories of people blaming their pain.

"I am getting older."
"I have a bad back, bum knee, tense neck, and weak ankles."
"I injured my back playing football when I was running, from sitting too much, from always being in the front of the computer."
"I injured it by deadlifting 400 lbs."
"I injured it from picking up a pencil."
"I slept on it wrong; I have an old crappy mattress."
"My pillow is too high, too low, too soft, too hard."
"My mom and dad also had a bad back. It must be in my genes."

Here's my story:

I was an athlete my entire life, loving sports that incorporated my natural speed and agility. I began sprinting in middle school and made the high school varsity team during my freshman year in 2003, running the 400-meter dash, which was quite a feat because I am only five feet, seven inches tall, and was racing against individuals way over six feet tall.

It was a hot and dry Thursday afternoon in April of 2003 in Miami, FL. We were on the last sprint of the day, preparing for a track meet the following day. I was exhausted but used my last bit of willpower when tragedy struck. As I took it up a notch too high, approaching the finish line of a 200-meter sprint, I felt a sudden sharp and crippling pain in my lower-right back and immediately crashed to the ground in tears.

I was **embarrassed** (I went to an all-boys Catholic school, and it's not particularly cool for a fifteen-year-old to cry in practice). I was **terrified** (did I break my back, herniate a disc, or tear through my spinal cord?) and **angry at myself** (I should've stretched more). I was helped and carried by two other athletes to my athletic trainer, who recommended I immediately see an orthopedic spine specialist to get an MRI.

My MRI showed two herniated discs (L4-L5 and L5-S1). The MD prescribed pain medications, ordered me to stop all weightlifting, and to never bend my spine forward because that would potentially deteriorate my herniations even further. Worst of all, he suggested that I should consider surgery because if I was in a car accident or lifted something poorly, it could cause a spinal cord injury resulting in paraplegia.

**Side note: Years later, I discovered this is physically impossible from disc herniations, but you can only imagine the fear that took over.**

This marked the beginning of a grueling eight-year journey with chronic lower-back pain. Every insecurity I've ever had in my life took over my mind as I became a **shell** of who I was before the injury.

My personality turned quiet and reserved. I could not sit still in school, constantly fidgeting due to my pain worsening if I would sit or stand longer than ten minutes. I couldn't concentrate on the material I was trying to learn. The pain would greet me every single morning the moment I'd wake up and prevent me from falling asleep comfortably every single night. I was irritable, depressed, and in constant worry and fear that the longer I bore this pain, the worse I was making my condition.

I never took the pain meds but followed the doctor's advice on never bending my spine to a neurotic degree. When I say I never bent my spine, I mean NEVER (which I later discovered was one of the main reasons I developed eight years of chronic pain).

A month after my injury, the intensity of my pain (on a 0–10 scale) was on average a five or six, which would escalate to an eight or nine every time I would run, play basketball, or weightlift, performing every single lift with a hyper-arched spine to stay as far away from the bent position as possible.

I was afraid to bend over and herniate my disc even worse. But I was also terrified of getting spinal surgery, knowing the research showed that only 20 percent of candidates with low back pain improve after getting surgery.

I was getting stiffer, more frustrated, and more depressed about my condition.

I tried a chiropractor, who adjusted me twice a week for a couple of months, with minimal relief. I tried massages and traditional physical therapy (electric stimulation, ultrasounds, basic hamstring stretches, machine exercises to "strengthen" the muscles that would support my back). All of these methods would relieve my pain temporarily, but NOTHING ever stuck.

This led me to pursue a career path for a Doctorate in Physical Therapy for two main reasons:

1. To fix my back
2. To be able to fix anyone

I received my bachelor's degree from Florida International University, studied Health Sciences, and was on the fast track to PT school. I started working at a PT clinic, learning the basics of how muscles work, and decided that I would like to become a certified personal trainer specializing in functional exercises and core exercises to at least help my clients prevent low back pain.

I fell in love with the human body and was fascinated by how muscles work together in an integrated manner. I was highly motivated and finished my undergraduate studies in three years because, in my mind, that was the only way I would fix myself. I was accepted to the University of Miami Physical Therapy School in 2009.

During my second year of PT school, I signed up for an optional weekend elective called "Foundations of Pilates for Rehabilitation" taught by a physical therapist named Brent Anderson.

I had no clue what Pilates was at the time, other than that it was usually done by women and didn't get you strong and powerful. I was only into powerlifting and bodybuilding but decided to give it a try.

Thank God, I had nothing better to do that weekend because that class completely altered how I viewed the body and how an efficient body is designed to move.

The standard way of viewing the body is very robotic and mechanical. If the knee hurts, strengthen and stretch the muscles of the knee. This is how most people view the human body and how I had treated my low back up until that point.

The class blew my mind and helped me "unlearn" everything I knew about the body up until that point.

It introduced me to the concept of viewing the body from a **holistic** perspective and the very real **mind-body** connection.

I learned that "pain memory" works just like "muscle memory," and we develop poor subconscious movement strategies and muscle compensations that **initially** protect us from pain but **ultimately** keep us locked in pain.

I learned about the immense power of the mind when it comes to the story it creates about your pain and the belief you have about the cause of your pain. This ties into your identity, preserving you in a guarded and protective state, making it impossible to get out of pain. I learned how the emotions of stress, fear, and worry act as a constant poison-drip to this vicious cycle of continuous tension in the body and mind, which continue to reinforce our beliefs about the reasons we are in pain.

I learned that our entire body is connected via a web-like connective tissue called fascia, which essentially acts as a full body suit. It runs superficially to the skin and as deep as the bone and connects the toes all the way up to the head. Restrictions in the fascia found above, below, in front, or behind can continue to cause the cycle of pain instead of the initial injury or the diagnosis.

In less than three months, I was completely pain-free.

During the next year, I immersed myself in Pilates, Yoga, breathing exercises, movement methods, how to calm the nervous system, salsa dancing, meditation, and self-contemplation.

I truly enjoyed running for the first time in my life. I learned how to "feel" music and have fun dancing. Weightlifting was no longer painful. I was more agile while playing basketball. I felt lighter on my feet when I walked. I was integrated and liberated. I was in shock that this wasn't general knowledge and that so many people were suffering from unnecessary and debilitating pain, being addicted to pain meds, and getting surgeries for something that can be treated by making a few intelligent adjustments to how we view and move our body.

What came to me as a complete bonus was the presence of mind and natural joy in my spirit that came along with it.

Since then, I've dedicated my life to teaching all the principles I learned from these mind-body methods and treating and viewing the body from a holistic perspective.

I was lucky enough to find a job right out of PT school at a clinic that viewed the body from a similar perspective, and I was able to work with individuals one-on-one from the start. I learned more about people's fears and frustrations, and I had the freedom to explore and utilize the principles I learned to see what exercises, movements, relaxation techniques, and beliefs require to create optimal results in the least period of time.

After a couple of years, I co-founded a fitness and Pilates studio called Sensory Fitness, combining the cardiovascular benefits of high-intensity-interval training with the mobility and restorative benefits of Pilates. I also own a cash-based PT practice called Rehab Lab where I work with individual clients, taking them from pain to performance. I am currently in the process of developing an online curriculum called

*Flowspace*, which merges meditation and mobility to teach individuals how to best approach and eliminate tension and weakness in the problem areas of their body.

Physical therapists are just now beginning to pay attention to the effects that the mind, deeply held beliefs, and emotions play in contributing to chronic pain.

I treat holistically because it brings empowering results in the fastest way possible.

We were designed to have a fully integrated body and mind, and our emotions have the power to either adapt to our circumstances or keep us locked in purgatory.

I am now considered a therapist, coach, a trainer, an "angel," and a miracle-worker by those whom I have treated.

I merely teach people how to reduce fear and reclaim the connection between their body, mind, and soul.

My concepts and principles are simple, but they are all-encompassing.

If you are currently dealing with pain, it all boils down to this.

You can continue to view your body and pain from a perspective of FEAR or begin to switch to a perspective of FREEDOM.

Fear is your brain's innate built-in system. Your brain is here to PROTECT your body and you from dying. Your brain doesn't care if you are pain-free, happy, and thriving.

FREEDOM is ultimately up to you. There has to be a conscious and courageous choice to free your body through intelligent movement, calming your mind to its natural state of presence, and committing to the daily practice of expanding your spirit through growth, love, and connection.

I know you have the power to make this commitment to yourself. **Your body has an infinite potential to heal itself but only if you allow it to.** I can't wait to meet you on the other side.

*"Most of us have two lives. The life we live, and the unlived life within us. Between the two, stands Resistance."*[18]
—Steven Pressfield

## BIOGRAPHY

After suffering a serious lower back injury at the age of fifteen, Guillermo was plagued with chronic low back pain every single day for eight years. At this point, Guillermo made a commitment to get himself out of pain. He received his Doctorate in Physical Therapy at the University of Miami and immersed himself in a variety of therapeutic movement and relaxation concepts that helped him move better and eventually get out of pain without any surgical intervention. Since then, he has dedicated his life to helping thousands of people get out of pain despite their hopeless diagnosis. Considered a therapist, coach, and a miracle worker by those he has treated, Guillermo implements the same holistic movement and mindset concepts that helped him to permanently erase unnecessary pain and get people back to living their best life. He currently resides in Miami, FL, where he owns a fitness studio and a concierge physical therapy practice.

Contact Guillermo De Novi via http://www.rehablabmiami.com

---

18   "Steven Pressfield Quotes," BrainyQuote (Xplore), accessed March 30, 2021, https://www.brainyquote.com/quotes/steven_pressfield_679153#:~:text=Steven%20Pressfield%20Quotes&text=Most%20of%20us%20have%20two%20lives%3A%20the%20life%20we%20live,Between%20the%20two%20stands%20Resistance.

CHAPTER 16

# What Now?

*By Jacob Long*

Have you ever taken a step back and taken a look at your life? No, I mean really taken a hard look at your life? It had been a few months since college ended, and normally I would have been headed back to school. Instead, I was lying on my bed, watching the ceiling fan spin in circles. All I could think to myself was, how did I get here? In the past, I had heard people say, "you are where you are supposed to be." Even the thought of someone telling me this made me mad. I wasn't supposed to be in this situation. I had dreams and goals that I was supposed to be living out at that very moment. Instead, I was broken, lost, and in a depression that seemed more insurmountable every day. It felt as if life had shattered the idea of the person I thought I was going to be, and I kept trying to put the pieces back together, but I never had them all. I took a hard look at my life and realized I had failed.

It all started when I was a kid playing sports. I was pretty good for my age and always played on teams with kids that were older than me. The more I played, the more I realized I wanted to play professional baseball. I traveled the country playing some of the best teams in the country with the expectation of going pro. After every training session, practice, and game, the image in my head of what it would be like when I made it to the Big Leagues became clearer. The smell of the grass, the roar of the crowd, and the feel of the red laces rolling across my fingers. I had imagined it so many times I knew exactly what it was going to be like. After all, if you believe it, you can achieve it, right? Not this time, folks.

Growing up in Colorado, playing baseball year-round wasn't a possibility. So, in high school, I played basketball during the winter. At the beginning of my sophomore season, during a scrimmage, I made a pass up the court to a teammate, and the defender who was trying to block the ball hit my arm and it slid in and out of place. Instantly I knew something was wrong. I might as well have been punched in the stomach because that's how painful it felt. I tried to lie to myself and make myself believe it would be okay. Those lies became impossible to believe when the doctor told me I tore my labrum and would need it surgically repaired. After many ups and downs, I was able to get back to playing baseball in high school and in college too. While I am grateful for the opportunity to continue playing, I knew I would never be the player I was before surgery or the one I could have been. I spent the last six years of my baseball career knowing in the back of my head that baseball would be over for me after college. Even still, there was a flicker of hope deep down that remained. When it was time to hang 'em up for the last time, that flicker died out, and with it, the persona I thought I was, did too.

Believe and you will achieve. I believed in my future and visualized it so much that I had begun to live a life that wasn't mine yet. As naive as it might sound, in a way, it felt as if the future was set in stone, and I just had to wait until it became mine. While believing that it is possible is key to achieving your dreams, sometimes things happen that are completely outside our control. Life takes over, throws you a curveball, and you have to ask yourself, now what?

Day after day, I would find myself staring at that fan. As I looked up at the spinning blades, I would get lost inside my own head. It was like a maze that never had an ending. I would always end up right back where I started. After months of this, I began to realize that this brokenness and depression was never about me not reaching my goals of playing in the MLB. It stemmed from my loss of identity. I didn't know who the real me was anymore. The days passed and I just kept sliding further down the slippery slope of depression. I would tell myself that I had no reason to be depressed. There are people in this world that have struggles far beyond what any of us could imagine, and I am depressed because a lofty dream I had didn't come true? Ironically, the worse I felt for being selfish for being depressed, the more depressed I became. It felt like I was taken over by a wave of emotion that trapped me tumbling in the undertow. No matter how hard I tried, I couldn't reach the surface.

In what felt like a final attempt to escape this cycle, I turned to medication. For weeks I took medication in the hopes of feeling better but instead, I felt nothing. To be honest, I was more scared of not feeling anything than I was of being depressed. As strange as it sounds, I would have rather felt the pain of depression because at least I knew I was alive. On the medication, I felt completely comatose. So, what now?

Knowing something had to change, I thought about all the drive and determination I had while playing baseball. What pushed me through all the tough times was the motivation to play pro ball. At this point in my life, I had no motivation. So, I went looking for some. After reading pages and pages of motivational quotes and stories, I realized that our pain only hurts as bad as we let it. This doesn't mean that all the pain we endure in our life is made up in our heads. Without a shadow of a doubt, everyone faces mental and emotional traumas, but that initial pain will subside. The pain we continually feel is the result of us reliving this pain in our head over and over again. One of the quotes that really stuck out to me was, "it's okay to be disappointed, but it is not okay to be discouraged." I suddenly realized that when my journey as a baseball player ended, it was okay for me to be disappointed, but I allowed it to consume me, and I became discouraged.

Eventually, I found the motivation to be what seemed like "normal" again, but those moments were fleeting. All too often, I felt paralysis by analysis, thinking so much about what I wanted my life to be in the end that I never figured out how to take the first step. All I knew was that I wanted to be successful. I had no idea what this "success" looked like or how I would get there. When my baseball career was over, one of the most difficult things I dealt with was feeling like I had failed the people who had worked so hard to help me reach my dreams. More than anything, I wanted them to be proud of the person I became. I didn't realize it at the time, but that was all the motivation I needed. Motivation, however, is temporary, it is an external influence that can get you started, but it will never get you out of the lowest lows on your journey to success. So I took that seed of motivation and turned it into my "why." Your why is that internal spark that nobody can take from you. No matter what you do or where you go, your why will be there holding you accountable, pushing you forward. I found out my why is making a positive impact on as many people as I can.

I still had to decide what to do, though—even knowing my "why," I didn't know how I would achieve success in a practical, tangible way in my day to day life. So I went back to my roots. Growing up watching my sisters play softball, I fell in love with the game. Having good friends that played, I got my foot in the door coaching softball. When I started, I never imagined that coaching competitive travel softball would make me feel successful because, at the time, I thought wealth and fame were the only things that made people successful. But it was a job that was fulfilling and that I was good at. After a tough year, this was enough for me. I didn't know that it was the first stepping stone on my path towards true success.

With every tournament that passed, the girls were growing right in front of me. The more we played, the more we won, and I could see all of the skills I had shown them during practice play out on the field, helping them achieve their goals. At the end of our first season, we took 4$^{th}$ place at nationals. I couldn't put into words how proud I was of what they had accomplished, both on and off the field. Beyond practical skills to improve their game, I really wanted to teach the girls life lessons. It was important to me to share things that have made me stumble along my journey and what I learned from them so that my players don't have to struggle with the same things. What I didn't expect was that in these teachable moments with them, they taught me far more than I could have taught them. My team didn't know it, but that summer, they taught me what true success really is. They taught me that when you educate and share your knowledge, you leave a positive mark on the lives of others that will last forever.

Just like I taught my players, the lessons you learn on the field will prepare you for life. So I took what my players taught me and started implementing it off the field. In college, I majored in business, and if nothing else, those four years taught me how to problem-solve. After all, that is what businesses do. They solve problems. Before coaching, I wouldn't have thought to combine my degree with education; I wasn't a teacher. Then, I realized that I could use my knowledge to help others solve their problems, specifically when it comes to financial literacy and self-sufficient investing. Now I "coach" off the field too, helping individuals grow financially, which allows them to better their communities with education, empowerment, and unity.

When my day comes, and I take my last breath on this earth, the players I coach might not remember me, and that's okay. Even if I don't live on in their memories, I hope to live on in the lessons I instilled in them. The same can be said for my financial literacy business partners. If I am able to positively impact their lives and communities by helping them achieve their goals, I am successful. They may not remember me, but my success is in them owning their own homes, building generational wealth, and passing on the education I provided them to members of their community. The beautiful thing about success is that there is no right way to do it. It looks different for each of us. I find success in making a positive impact on the lives of as many people as I can. You might feel successful by becoming rich and famous, and there is nothing wrong with that. You are on your journey, not mine. But no matter what success is to you, take a good hard look at your life and figure out what success is to you. Your why will get you there.

# BIOGRAPHY

Jacob Long has been a coach and educator for the last six years. He provides aspiring collegiate athletes advanced instruction and educates investors on how to be self-sufficient traders. Jacob finds success through seeing his athletes and business partners reach their goals. If he isn't on the field with his athletes or working with business partners on the charts, he spends his time with family and friends.

Contact Jacob Long via https://linktr.ee/Jacob_Long

CHAPTER 17

# Deep-Rooted Success From Self-Empowerment

*By Jannette Tomamao*

The Philippines is famous for being a source of migrant workers. Parents leave their families to go abroad in the hope of giving their children a better future. I spent much of my childhood growing up without my mom and dad; they left when I was ten years old. My parents leaving us was already bad enough, but the worst was when my dad abandoned us financially and left our family broken.

**Recollection of My Childhood**

On weekends, kids in our neighborhood would be excited as they would have the privilege of playing in the mud until their hearts were filled with joy and they would become oblivious of time—but not for the naive but determined ten-year-old girl I was. Playing on weekends was seldom an option. Money was scarce, so I would find a way to make some for my school allowance the following week.

*My business mindset had its roots here.*

My grandparents planted a Bilimbi tree, commonly called *Kamias* in the Philippines, and "cucumber tree" or "tree sorrel" in English. This prolific tree had been around for as long as I can remember. It is still in my grandparent's backyard. At five in the morning, I would climb the tree and gather its fruits. I would need to deliver it to market by six o'clock; otherwise, I would miss the chance of selling my *Kamias* fruit to the vegetable traders who would pay inversely proportional to their profit. Together with my sister, we would walk to town, helping each other carry the weight of the produce. As we headed to town, I poignantly recall I wore odd slippers, given that was all I had. We had no extra money to buy a new pair. I did not complain. I accepted my state.

My weekend didn't end there. I would trade my time as a helper at my aunt's meat shop, for which I would earn twenty pesos for the day. I would feel extremely delighted to receive my hard-earned money. It taught me the value of money and prudence.

My hands would be sore, itchy, and cut up due to constant exposure to pig's blood, tissue juice, and water. But it was okay; I knew that they would heal by the following weekend. Some weekends, during planting season, I would help my uncles who tended a farm; we would plant vegetables from 7 a.m. to 5 p.m. I would endure the heat of the sun. I had several other means of earning money and it was a damn hard job. I felt like I was so underprivileged every single time. I made a firm conviction and promised myself that life would become better, and that this was temporary.

*"Always remember that your present situation is not your final destination."*[19]
—Zig Ziglar

I was a student who faced many financial obstacles that affected me psychologically and socially during my high school and college years. I developed a self-limiting belief that money was always scarce and that the poor remain poor forever. In schools, we were not taught to deal with the stressors that life brought; therefore, I got to choose my outcome.

---

19 "A Quote by Zig Ziglar," Goodreads (Goodreads), accessed March 31, 2021, https://www.goodreads.com/quotes/915549-always-remember-that-your-present-situation-is-not-your-final.

When I was in high school, I would make and sell ice *lollies*. During my college days, I would make and sell sandwiches to my co-interns. I would sell beauty products in between classes. Not only did I gain small profits, which I would use as capital the following day, but also the respect and admiration of my mentors and classmates. Finally, I began to feel and understand the meaning of victory. I would never stop selling, even after I had my first paid job. A voice deep within my heart would contradict my belief, whispering that I was made for more and deserved more. My childhood experiences empowered me. I became resilient and courageous. I owe it to my childhood for the woman I am now, and I wouldn't trade it for anything.

I vividly remember how hard I would study because I wanted to get out of my situation. I developed and honed my grit. I would miss my mama; she would send just enough money to pay our school fees. Daddy forgot about us and didn't send money for a long time. I will be eternally thankful to my mother for all her love and sacrifice. She chose to leave, not because she wanted to, but because she needed to. I admired her courage to face a rather challenging and lonely life abroad.

Living without parents taught me to become more responsible and self-reliant. Nonetheless, to this day, I am grateful for my aunts. They looked after us and housed us when we had neither a house nor parents to look after us and provide for our needs.

I strived even harder. I was convinced that life would be better after I graduated with a bachelor's degree; hence, I pursued it to the best of my ability. I wouldn't want to go back to the state of my childhood again, nor would I want my children to experience what I had been through. I had this burning desire within my soul that kept me motivated to finish my degree, even in the face adversity. During examinations, there were several occasions where I should have given up, not because I wasn't prepared to take the test, but because I was not allowed to do so due to the accounting clearance not being signed. This was because I had no money to pay for my tuition fees. There were countless times where I would write promissory notes because the allowance from my mama always came late. It was a hell of a state. I feared my situation, and worst of all, I was ashamed to admit it. This impacted my perspective; I developed self-doubt. I kept it to myself because I worried that my friends would laugh at me if they found out how poor I was. But I did not give up; I committed to finishing my bachelor's degree without any delay. I pushed my self-doubt away. I began to look up to people who hit rock bottom in their lives but were still able to reach the pinnacle of success.

In August of 1995, my third year in the university, I met the love of my life, my best friend, my soul mate, my motivation and inspiration. I started to see sunshine and rainbows. I became more passionate about finishing my degree. I became alive and happier. I am grateful to God and the Universe that our paths crossed, and I knew that he was the man with whom I would want to grow old and live a life of abundance and gratefulness. I found a man who believed in me, cared for my vulnerability, and accepted the person I was.

**How Did I Transform Self-Doubt and Self-Limiting Belief into Self-Empowerment?**

Self-empowerment, in general, is taking control of our own lives, making positive choices, and setting goals. We have to develop the value of understanding our strengths and weaknesses and believing in our potential. When you're self-empowered, you get plenty done, which will massively help you become more self-confident and healthier in mind and body.

When it comes to believing, you can craft your success and shape your destiny. The most effective way to do so is to have a *self-conversation*. Self-talk is the single most important conversation that one should care about. It lets you analyze your "why." Why do you matter? What is your true purpose?

I use this technique to overcome self-doubt and to develop a positive mindset which, more often than not, results in the state of euphoria, of feeling empowered. It is like a muscle that I need to grow and develop by using it every day.

I recently adopted a coaching formula from the Coaching and Personal Development course I was undertaking at the time of writing this book. I thought it was a great framework to utilize when having a self-conversation. It is called the G.R.O.W. Success Formula.

**G-Goal:** *What is my goal? What outcome do I want to achieve? Why am I even alive?*

- When we mention goals, we usually think long-term. But really, goals can be broken into smaller tasks. Set your long-term goals (+10 years), medium goals (1–5 years), and short-term goals (1 day–1 year).
- Your short-term goals should be in sync with your long-term goals, for which you should foster discipline, consistency, and focus. With this guidance, you are more likely to succeed.
- Establish what you want to work towards.

**R-Resources:** *What the resources available to you that would help you achieve your goal?*

- Goals are more likely to be achieved with the right resources.
- Most of the time, we have readily available resources, but we are unaware of utilizing them effectively.
- Our resources can be external or internal. External ones are from our surroundings; they can come from physical objects. Internal ones come from within us; these could be our ideas or thoughts that we can cultivate and fertilize.

**O-Obstacles:** *What is stopping you from achieving your goal? What mindset barrier are you currently having?*

- These are the barriers, blocks, challenges, and problems that are present in your situation. It becomes easier to overcome these once you know what they are and how they present themselves.

**W-Work your way to move forward:** *What are you going to do to achieve your desired outcome? How are you going to make your goal a reality?*

- When you have a self-talk, you will be able to dissect a potential solution that could help move the needle in your life.
- Believe it can be done, and it is halfway through. Don't underestimate where your creative mind can take you. Eliminate "I can't do," "It is impossible," and "It won't work."
- Celebrate every small win because these small victories will fuel your desire to do and achieve more.

> *"Nothing is impossible, the word itself says I'm possible."*[20]
> —Audrey Hepburn

When you follow this G.R.O.W. framework during self-talk, you will have a structured, step-by-step solution to achieve success, eliminate self-doubt, and be the person you want to be. It will help you keep a mindset of success and kill procrastination. It will catapult you to where you want to be.

Talking to yourself will feel, sound, and look crazy when you are not used to it, but believe me that this works like magic. If you want to be successful, you may want to try it. Positive self-talk can enormously help a person's attitude and mindset, which sequentially leads to improved relationships with others, higher self-esteem, and a better perspective.

There is no specific time to practice it. Still, I find it more effective when done in the morning during my meditation routine, and in the evening during my gratitude routine. The morning self-talk allows me to visualize a positive outcome for the day; it helps me focus on my goals and desired outcomes, thereby creating a more productive day. The evening self-talk allows me to analyze whether or not I could accomplish my goal and reflect on whether I made a positive impact on the world. I record

---

20  "Audrey Hepburn Quotes," BrainyQuote (Xplore), accessed March 31, 2021, https://www.brainyquote.com/quotes/audrey_hepburn_413479.

my daily success (even small wins) in my journal. This allows me to stay motivated. Truly, my childhood experience of growing in a poor family taught me invaluable lessons on self-discipline and self-empowerment. I'd say I disagree with the concept of luck, but I firmly believe that you are the variable to your own success, and you can manipulate your fate.

> *"Empowerment is never about blame;*
> *it is about taking personal responsibility."*[21]
> —Bryan McGill

Reading till the end, you might be in search of inspiration and strategy. Now, **I challenge you to empower yourself to succeed…**

## BIOGRAPHY

A Native Filipina, Jannette Tomamao has a degree in Medical Technology. Her passion for empowering parents who are stressed, over-worked, and undervalued led her to become a Business Mentor, Transformational Mindset Coach, and an NLP Practitioner. She attributes her strong character to her childhood, and her mantra is "I am what I chose to become."

Contact Jannette Tomamao via https://linktr.ee/jannette_tomamao1976

---

21 Bryant McGill, "Empowerment Is Never about Blame; It Is about Taking Personal Responsibility.," Official Site of Bryant McGill, accessed March 31, 2021, https://bryantmcgill.com/quotes/empowerment-never-blame-taking-personal-responsibility/.

CHAPTER 18

# Adversity

*By John Kelly*

Adversity is when circumstances, and pretty much everything, go against you. These are hardships that you have to face head-on. They will strengthen you if you are resilient and work through them.

Growing up, my family was poor. My mother was a single parent who raised six children. She cleaned houses, and washed and ironed clothes for a living. She was a strict disciplinarian, which helped me later in life. One evening, after dinner, I did not clear the table and wash the dishes, even though it was my turn. Since no one told me to do my job, I went outside to play. When it was time to get to bed, no one mentioned anything about me not washing the dishes. I went to bed thinking I had gotten away not fulfilling my responsibility. Later that night, I awoke to a whipping with a switch. So, I had to get up and wash the dishes with whimpers and tears. That night, I learned that one needs to fulfill their responsibilities without needing to be told to do so.

At the age of twelve, I helped my mother with the family expenses by putting up and tearing down rides at the Kansas Free Fair. I also worked after school and on weekends at the local car wash. This enabled me to help with expenses and buy my clothes.

I enlisted for the Marine Corps when I was seventeen. This was a traumatizing experience. Imagine being screamed at, taking body shots, and being demoralized daily for twelve weeks. Everything you did was wrong, and you were punished for it. For example, if you were bitten by a sand flea and killed it, you had to give it a proper burial. The flea was put in a matchbox, and you had to dig a hole six feet deep and bury it. I learned to persevere and became the platoon guide. I was motivated, developed ingenuity, and learned to become a team player and never quit. My perseverance made one of five Marines who were meritoriously promoted.

After finishing up boot camp, I went to school to be an electronics repairman. After my schooling, I was assigned to Beaufort, South Carolina Marine Corps Air Station. There, I received two promotions and orders to Vietnam.

Serving in Vietnam brought about an onset of personal involvement. Every Marine has two MOS's. The first MOS is an infantryman, better known as a Grunt. Grunts are the Marines that do the actual hands-on fighting. Therefore, every Marine, regardless of their MOS, had to go to the front line. The second MOS is a specialty job that provided support whenever the Grunts needed to complete their job. All I will say about Vietnam is that you did whatever was necessary for you and your team to survive. I learned a valuable lesson about money while serving in Vietnam. While we were in the bush, we were cold, hot, dirty, thirsty, and hungry. We could not buy a bath, a drink of water, a soda, or a hamburger. We could not do any of these things even though we had a pocketful of money. I learned that money can't always buy what you need. I received my last promotion and orders to go stateside after my thirteen months of tour duty. I was assigned to San Diego MCRD and was honorably discharged five months later.

After I was discharged, I got married and was expecting my first child. I was in dire need of employment. Since I had worked in the electronics field, I applied for a position at a production plant. After interviewing for the position, the person conducting the interview threw my application into the trash. I was livid and told him that he could have at least waited until I was gone. Another interviewer heard the commotion and came out to see what was going on. I told him the other interviewer could have waited until I was gone to throw my application into the trash. He said he couldn't hire me for the electronic position, but he could hire me for an industrial position in the plant. I agreed.

After working in this position for several months, my machine operator asked me if I had applied for an apprenticeship program. I replied that I had not, and he suggested that I do so. I went to the office to apply for the apprenticeship program and was told they were not accepting further applications. The next day, my machine operator enquired about my application. After filling him in on what I was told, he told me that was not true and that I should talk to the head of the program. I did as he suggested and was told that the program was still open and that my name would be considered in the selection process. As a result, I was selected into the apprenticeship program and later completed it. I learned that one needed to go to the source if they sought the correct information.

The maintenance department was comprised of "good ol' boys." I was not such a person and was pretty much an outcast to the journeyman. They would leave me in the break area, saying they were going to use the bathroom, but instead go to work. The supervisor would come by and ask me why I was not on the job, to which I would tell them my journeyman was in the bathroom. The supervisor told me the truth. I learned, then, to do whatever I needed to do to be on the hip of my journeyman. Wherever he went, I went. An old navy veteran electrician took me under his wing and taught me what I needed to know. As a result, I became very proficient at my job.

After people began buying imported products, I lost my job. The company I worked for laid me off.

The federal government gave everyone who was laid off a stipend for twelve months, which provided them income until they found a job. Instead of playing cards and dominos, I decided to pursue a master's degree. After getting accepted into the MBA program, my adviser did not want me to take as many hours as I needed to take because he thought the workload might be a bit too much for me. I had enough money for only one year's tuition, so I had to finish my program within those twelve months. I completed the program and made my adviser proud.

After earning my MBA degree, I applied for several jobs but only received a stack of thank you letters. I had a family to feed, so I went to work for the state as an electrician. My plan was to work as an electrician and later apply for an administrative position. Again, I received only a stack of thank you letters. One day, on my way to the shop, I heard my supervisor tell someone over the phone that I was not a good employee. I realized then why I was getting that stack of thank you letters. So, I used the department head as a reference, and I received an administrative position. After working in my new position for several months, my supervisor and I were having communication issues. I asked her for an audience, and she told me I was not following instructions. I asked her to give me instructions in writing to protect both her and me. I told her if I received written instructions, she could not say that I did not do the job as per the said instructions. She replied, saying that I was an intelligent individual and she was not going to spoon-feed me. So, I climbed up the chain of command and told everyone that we had a communication problem. The HOD called me to his office and said I was terminated. We sat there for twenty minutes, and I told him if there was nothing further to be discussed that this meeting was adjourned. If I would have raised my voice or displayed unprofessional conduct, he would have grounds to fire me for insubordination. I left his office and called the HR department. After having told them I was terminated, I enquired about my next step. They told me I could not be terminated because a person needed to have two unsatisfactory evaluations in a row—I had none! So, I requested for a grievance meeting. When I went to get the files to support my position, I was told the files were all moved, and I did not have access to them. I had some files on my desk that were not finalized, so I used those to support my position against every claim they made, rather than waste my words. I was graded after every audit, and the lowest grade I received was a ninety-two. After the panel made their decision, I was told I was given a 100 percent rating; I went back to work.

I applied for and received an administrative position in another department. Everything went well until people started to complain that I was never in my office, to which I explained that I was responsible for the northern half of the state. A portion of my job description was to receive and resolve complaints or issues the department received. I explained I had to be in the field to better understand the issues. I questioned whether my work was substandard and was told I had received excellent evaluations. I called a meeting and explained everything that I did. Everyone agreed they were unaware of the amount of work I was doing. Yet, people still complained that I was never in the office.

Later, the department reorganized, and I lost my position. As a result, I decided to retire after eighteen years of service. About a month after I retired, I received a call and was told that a position was available and I wouldn't have to give an interview. I decided that I had enough workplace adversity, and I was now in a position to control my destiny. Therefore, I respectfully declined the position.

Overcoming adversity is a learned behavior. When you go through an adverse time in your life, you have to navigate around or over the obstacle and use it as a learning experience. Some people throw up their hands and say 'Woe is me' when they encounter adverse conditions. Every time I encountered adverse conditions, I found ways to overcome them. I focused on the positive aspects of every challenge I faced. This gave me the confidence, strength, and flexibility to overcome every obstacle. When facing adversity, we have the choice to either do nothing or do something to overcome what we're facing. Our personal and professional growth depends on how we respond to adversity. This will define who we are as a person and allow us to survive hardships.

## BIOGRAPHY

John Kelly grew up the oldest of six children in a single-parent home. He was looked upon as the head figure of the family at a young age. As a result, he learned how to relate well with adults and other children. He also learned to be ambitious, generous, and thoughtful.

His goal is to assist others with achieving their personal development as easily as possible. In addition to helping others achieve their personal development, he inspires them to use adversity to their advantage. Helping others to achieve their personal development gives him great satisfaction.

His greatest achievement was obtaining a bachelor's degree. He had to juggle a full-time job, working a 48-hour week, being a single parent, and carrying 12–15 hours per semester.

He loves being a grandparent. He gets to spoil his grandkids and great-grandkids and then send them home to their parents.

Contact John Kelly via https://Linktr.ee/mrjkelly2

CHAPTER 19

# The Hero's Journey

*By John Kennedy*

Growing up, I was taught what is probably still being taught. Go to school, get good grades, go to college, find a good job, work hard, get promoted, retire at sixty-five (on 40 percent of what you earned), and kick back and relax because "you've earned it." No one ever told me was "it" was.

My Marketing degree took me to the second largest employer in California, next to the state government: Pacific Bell. I worked there as a communications consultant for two years, selling business-phone systems and PBXs. Right up my alley . . . NOT! Then, I got a call from another company of interest to me: United Airlines. For their marketing department in Chicago? Nope, as a supervisor for their narrow-body flight kitchen at SFO! What the f***? But I was told, 'Just get in with the company and move up later.' So, I did.

It was hell from the first day! We cranked out 9000 meals for over 130 flights a day. God help you if you caused the delay for any of those 130 flights! I worked the day shift for three months, then the swing shift for the next three months, and then the dreaded graveyard shift for the following three months, until our little Napoleon manager decided to switch to six-month rotations. This meant three more months on graveyard.

I wanted out quickly. But in the history of that kitchen, no supervisor had been promoted out in less than two years, and I was only on my seventh month! That was all I needed! Fortunately, our European Executive Chef, his German sous chefs, and I hit it off really well. I went to Chef Wolfsheimer and said, "Chef, I need to get out of here. Will you teach me as much as you can, as fast as you can, to make me more valuable and promotable?"

Quick side note. I learned nothing about cooking growing up. Mom, bless her heart, cooked almost everything, it seemed, in a pressure cooker. So, the only culinary "color" I knew was gray, and the only "texture" I knew was "you can eat it with a spoon." But I digress.

Chef agreed. But because it was a union kitchen, the union had to agree. They decided that I could work with the chef and cooks after my management shift, without pay, so as not to take away a job from the non-management union cooks. DONE! So, for more than four months, I worked my graveyard shift and then changed clothes and worked an extra six to eight hours during the day shift to be under the watchful tutelage of the executive chef.

It worked! I was promoted out of the flight kitchen one day short of a year with the company! My next stop was the catering division, under a man who was to end up being the best person for whom I've ever worked! I could write another book on what Joe McDonough did for me and the other guys who worked for him. Maybe I will. Joe gave all of us the reigns to do our own thing, to push the envelope, be different, bend the rules when it made sense, and to try to find a better way if it would better the company. I certainly did my part for about five years, including building a flight kitchen in Ixtapa, Mexico, in a former house of ill repute. Joe knew the minute he saw the completed facility. He simply said, "Let's keep that part our little secret."

Then, a sales position opened up in San Diego. I knew the sales rep who was to leave. He convinced me to interview for his position, which included being United's professional sports rep. I did as advised, and I ended up getting accepted. Doing so put me in closer touch with the community since I was out of the kitchen and into businesses. I joined Rotary; I flew with the San Diego Chargers for seven years as the sports rep, including during the coldest game in NFL history in Cincinnati, where windchill was fifty-nine below at game time. I played golf with

Arnold Palmer, flew with the Padres Baseball Club, met Ray Kroc, and got involved with the Muscular Dystrophy Association. I put together a fundraising promotion with United Airlines and local travel agents that netted MDA in San Diego $10,000. At the time, that was the largest corporate donation to MDA in San Diego. It got the attention of MDA corporate and United Corp, who had me fly to Las Vegas and present the $10,000 check to Jerry Lewis on TV. It wouldn't be my last time presenting Jerry a check because I was President of the San Diego/Imperial County chapter of MDA and a board member for fourteen years.

My career with United changed again when I became District Sales Manager for a brief time. I was then approached by a group of former high-level airline executives who launched a new airline company out of San Jose. They wanted me as the Director of Food Services. It was an extremely risky move, but I was vested in United and would have retirement pay later down the road, so I took it. I commuted every day from San Diego to San Jose and back—500 miles each way. Thank goodness I had friends at PSA. Sadly, after about six to seven months, we shut down the attempt. Shortly thereafter, I went to work for another start-up airline that would fly between LAX and HNL, and SFO and HNL. I became Director of Sales. While we got off the ground and got the business running, I sensed something shady going on. I did some behind-the-scenes research and found out it was more than just shady. They had just asked me to fly up to SFO and explain to the press that our forced cancellations were caused by constant mechanical errors from our maintenance contractors when, in fact, the planes were fine. It was the owners' lack of payments to the leasing company that was grounding the planes. Instead of flying to SFO, I called my dad, a Superior Court judge, and asked him if I was crazy to do it? He simply asked, "Could you live with your decision to remain on board?" I tendered my resignation instead. The company toppled like a tower of cards a couple of weeks later—so as did my United retirement after the company declared bankruptcy!

My marketing degree, and varied experiences, brought me follow-up careers. My next designation was GM of a gourmet dessert company in San Diego, which I handled for two and a half years. From the owner, I learned two valuable lessons that I've never stopped utilizing: firstly, how to make delicious cheesecake and mousse; and secondly, how NOT to treat people. But despite growing the business from $2 million a year to $4 million a year, I was miserable. I was approached by a friend of a friend who was going to import coffee from Mexico to the US—Mexico's second-best coffee brand. But he knew nothing about marketing. He offered me the position of president of the company. I met the owners of the coffee company, imported the coffee in, got it into the markets in LA and San Diego, got the US Army to purchase the coffee, and even came up with my own brand of coffee, that we blended in Hawaii with Kona beans, called Paradise Blend. Unfortunately, the owner began facing some serious personal problems, and the company was liquidated.

So naturally, like an idiot, I became a successful chef/owner of a deli/restaurant in my town. One day, I catered an affair at our community's new Performing Art Center and was impressed with the venue. My wife and I went out to dinner that night, exhausted from all the catering. I was staring down at my second scotch and soda, in deep thought, when my wife asked me what I was thinking about. I told her that it was such a great venue that I wanted to put on a concert there. She laughed and said those magic words, "You can't do that. You've never put on a concert. Besides, who would you get?" I kept starring at my cocktail when I blurted out, "It's right here. *This* is who!" She had no idea, but *Scotch and Soda* was a famous song of the famed Kingston Trio. She laughed again, saying, "You'll never get the Kingston Trio." That was music to my ears. I did four concerts with them over two years and donated $16,000 to MDA. Another trip to see Jerry.

From there, I became GM of a wholesale food distributor. Then I spent five years as an independent sales rep for a friend of mine in St. Louis, who sold refurbished telecom equipment, followed by a 10+ years career in the golf industry, which included owning my own custom club fitting studio in Carlsbad.

Out of nowhere, due to a debilitating health issue, I was forced to sell the studio. The day I signed the sales agreement, I was introduced to, and got involved with, network marketing—something I swore I'd never do simply because I pre-judged the industry and because I didn't know what I didn't know.

What immediately impressed me was that I was surrounded by so many positive-minded people. I was introduced to a company that focused not only on their products but on personal development—something that Corp America never touched on. While transitioning to network marketing, I met a wonderful gentleman in Kauai, Mark Januszewski, now a close friend, who teaches a course called *The Master Keys*. It literally changed my life.

I was introduced to the **Hero's Journey**. Hell, I had taken it so many times in my career and didn't even know it! I had been living it, going from the known to the unknown, being called to adventure with each opportunity, and stepping outside of my comfort zone numerous times. I faced challenges and temptations, but I also had helpers and mentors along the way who contributed to my revelations and transformations. I returned from each adventure a better, wiser person who was allowed to realize his potential. Call me Luke Skywalker, as he was faced with the same journey. He left the safety of the known to rescue Princess Leah and faced numerous challenges, but not without helpers like Hans Solo, R2D2, 3CPO, and others. And they all faced the Abyss yet fought through it and returned richer in many ways. Every movie ever made is about the Hero's Journey. Think about that!

The Hero's Journey taught me to permit myself to be successful in ways other than simply financial. Throughout all my years in various businesses, I didn't have a lot of money to show for all I had done. I must have failed because I have neither the material wealth nor the retirement that many of my friends have (many of whom took someone else's "prescribed" career paths). However, for the first time, I realized that I have ABUNDANCE in my life; and I can thank those who have challenged me and forced me to take action. *The Master Keys* also taught me that our subconscious makes all our decisions!

Did you know that your "subby" is as dumb as a sack of hammers, that it believes anything you tell it? It doesn't know the difference between $100 and $1 million. So, tell it you're going to earn $1 million! And your "subby" NEVER forgets . . . ever! Use that knowledge to your benefit. Write down what you desire and read it out loud twice or thrice a day. Your "subby" will get it done for you as mine did for me. Reading Napoleon Hill (*Think and Grow Rich*) and others, taught me that our thoughts are real. If they are said out loud with emotion for the Universe and subconscious to hear time and again, whatever it is you desire will physically manifest. I learned that dream boards are for adults as much as they are for grade school kids. Parents shouldn't tell their kids to stop daydreaming. In fact, they should ENCOURAGE it! I'm telling you: create a dream board for yourself and place it where you can see it every day! I have created a hashtag that I use all the time: #DreamBigActOnIt. Feel free to use it! My dream board worked. Me living in the house of my dreams in Maui proves it.

My latest challenge has been my speech which went south about four years ago. It's getting better each day because I'm constantly telling my "subby" and the Universe that it needs to improve. I refuse to accept anything less. Yes, I struggle on Zoom and phone calls, but that's not going to stop me. It's just another Hero's Journey challenge I embrace because the rewards are ultimately many. I'm not rich in fortune yet, but I am rich in experience, gratitude, friendships, and abundance. And I'm living the dream of the Hero's Journey. Embrace your Hero's Journey!

Success to me is accomplishing something I've set out to do from which others will benefit.

## BIOGRAPHY

John Kennedy's career has seen him hold several positions in business: Supervisor, Director of Food & Beverage, Director of Sales, Corp. President, GM, Chef/Owner, International Sales Manager, Assistant Golf Coach, Small Business Owner, Student, Mentor, Professional Sports Representative, and Network Marketer. His most prized title is Husband and Stepdad. Throughout John's career, he has made a conscious effort not to follow in someone else's path but to forge his own trail. Along the way, he's faced failures. But along with these, there have also been monumental successes, amazing life experiences, and revelations that he would have never experienced had he chosen the safe path. Based on his vast business knowledge in various fields, coupled with lessons learned from mentors he has met along his journey, John offers a surprising yet simple look at a method to unlock everyone's true potential.

Contact John Kennedy via https://linktr.ee/JohnK808

CHAPTER 20

# Solving The Rubik's Cube Of Network Marketing

*By Karyn Mahoney*

Ever feel like you are trapped in a Rubik's cube while trying to work out how to get through this journey of network marketing? That's how I felt for twenty plus years. It's a puzzle other people seem to be able to work out but not me.

I have joined many opportunities; some I've done well at and others not so well. I even became a manager and had a small team under me. My biggest achievement was being the No.1 New Manager for the year 2016 in my distributorship. I still hold the record for most sales in one week for a New Manager—$14K plus.

So, I worked out that not being successful must come down to me, but . . .

Did I even have the desire, motivation, or determination to get there?

After paying thousands of dollars over the years for mentors and coaches, why isn't success happening for me?

I read self-development books; I do all the training. Still, it wasn't working. I couldn't figure out why I wasn't a success yet!

The words "mindset" or "find your Why" drives me nuts: I don't have kids, so I don't really have that "why" parents seem to have. Yeah, I want the nice house and not having to worry about where the money is coming from to pay the bills. But I don't want to slave for someone else at a 9 to 5 job.

Mindset. Find your WHY. Blah! If it were that easy, wouldn't everyone be successful?

I joined a few other opportunities, each time thinking, "this will be the one, I know it!"

Then 2020 happened; my trip to Bali got canceled. That was okay—I could go without a holiday—but I could not stop thinking about my beautiful Bali family—Gday, my driver, his wife Arick (my Bali sister), and their kids—how they would survive with no work? How would they feed their kids? How would they pay the rent? I didn't sleep well because I knew that if they were struggling, then many others were too.

My best friend was also struggling to buy nappies for her little girl, toilet paper, wipes, and many other essentials she needed for her family. I recently made the decision to move interstate, so I was not there to help. I sent my best friend a voucher for an online store, so she could get what she needed.

I also took a collection up between family and friends to send Gday and Arick money to help them feed their family and loved ones, but that would not keep them going. And how many other families were and are still suffering?

Arick was about to have a baby, and they were so grateful for the money.

A few months later, their newborn baby ended up in hospital with a lung infection. That was scary, as Bali's hospitals and services are not as well-equipped as those here in Australia. Plus, I knew the cost would cripple the family, who struggled as it was.

Then Arick called me in tears; I could hear the fear in her voice. Not just for her baby but for her whole family. She told me they had already sold the car (Gday's pride and joy) and all the jewelry they owned. I could not sit and do nothing. Again, I did a collection drive and raised more money, so at least they could give the hospital some money and feed the family.

I cried myself to sleep that night, feeling so helpless. How could I help from here in Australia? How could I make a difference to people who are in need—I mean real need.

Then it hit me—I suddenly had my WHY!

After all these years, I now knew what my mentors and coaches meant when they talked about finding your WHY.

I want to create a legacy based on helping those in need and can't help themselves.

Something else I always wanted to do since having my own team in my direct sales business is to help entrepreneurs put into action what they learn. I had this vision of people from different companies all working together, sharing knowledge. I have a saying, "Knowledge Shared Is Power," which means helping each other out and learning from each other.

Something a lot of people do is attend training after training and look busy; it makes them feel like they are taking action. But are they really?

Now that I had my Why, suddenly, my mindset came along for the ride.

Mindset and your Why are everything; just keep looking until you find them. All the knowledge you gain in the meantime will come in handy, I can assure you. I am now enjoying my journey and not finding it so frustrating. Yes, there are still ups and downs, but the difference is that now I know I can get through them and that most successful people have been through them too.

It is a tough journey but worth it in the end.

Only those willing to work at the Rubik's cube will solve it. If you keep putting it aside, saying I can't do it, it's too hard, then it will be. Never give up, keep trying, keep learning. Once I work something out, I just want to show others how to do it.

It doesn't matter what others think, especially your family and friends. They love you so much they are fearful for you. People fear change—in themselves and others. They are fearful you will fail, but failing is required in this industry, several times if possible. It will make you more knowledgeable, more determined, and into someone to whom others can go when they feel like giving up, to show them it can be done.

Don't fear change, embrace it—fail forward!

When I got over worrying about how others perceive me, I got over my fear, started taking action, and began seeing results.

Taking action eliminates fear!

Surround yourself with like-minded people, those who understand your craziness and passion for achieving. Surround yourself with people who bring out the best in you and learn lessons from those who have already achieved what you want.

No coach is teaching anything new; success lies in how they put the information across and how you relate to it. Find coaches and mentors with whom you can relate. Keep looking until you find that coach and community that will support you one hundred percent.

The biggest change in my mindset was when I found the right mentors and community to support me.

Another piece to the Rubik's cube I needed to solve was acknowledging that people DO need to hear my story, my lesson, my WHY. Imagine if it helped them write their first book, make their first sale, or their first million!

Everything I experienced in my life gave me the strength to keep going when it got hard. Over the past twenty years, one of the hardest things was coming to terms with my partner committing suicide.

Then came a bad breakup with another long-term partner that caused me much anxiety.

Ten years of a near-perfect relationship, and then he changed dramatically. Then, there were two years of suffering, with him bordering on getting physically abusive and me realizing he was on ICE. I finally decided to leave. I packed a suitcase and stayed with one of my old bosses I was still close to. I didn't want my partner to harass my friends.

The hardest thing was: it was MY house, not his, but I had to leave!

Barry did start to harass my friends—going to my best friend's house and threatening her partner, whom he didn't even know. He went to another friend's house and harassed her tenant, as she had just moved interstate. He even found a list of names and addresses from a baby shower I had thrown for a friend and had gone to nearly every house on the list to find me. One of them called the police on him, and he was charged. But that did not stop him.

One day, not long after I left to go to work, I felt as though a car was following me but dismissed it as nothing more than an idiot driver. I went to pull into a park at the shops, and before I had a chance to get out of the car, I realized it was Barry. I took off quickly, but he followed me and tried to run me off the road. I was so scared. I called the police and told them I was being followed by an ex and was too scared to stop. They told me to put my hazard lights on and keep flashing my lights and honking my horn until I got to the police station. When I got there, I raced out of my car—Barry was right on my tail—and bolted into the police station. The police grabbed me and took me straight out the back and dealt with Barry screaming and yelling at me over the counter.

They did not charge him. Instead, they just let him go. I went back to my boss's house, but by now, Barry had found out where I was and was threatening them too. I thanked my boss and her husband, got in my car, and drove all night to my home state, back to my mum's.

I left MY house, my job, my friends, my life. I left with just a suitcase, and it was hell for the next year or so to get him out of MY house and out of my life. He would call me constantly—I don't know how many numbers I blocked or how many times I changed my number, but he always found a way to get it.

He would call my mum at her work daily, to the point she called me and said, "I can't handle this, Karyn." Uh, Mum, what do you think he is doing to me? I could not be held responsible for his actions, as I had left him.

So, after I finally got him out of my life, I was still left with depression and added anxiety.

The trauma of it all was so bad that I had to stop working as a debt collector and take some time out to heal.

I moved in with my aunt as her caregiver and started another direct selling business—I think my fourth or fifth by that time. And I was running a cleaning business at the same time. I did well for a time, but it didn't seem to be working out as with everything in my life. I was never consistent; I was never able to get that motivation.

Then my aunt suddenly died. I was devastated; she had been my rock. How would I ever get over her loss?

I thought it was the depression and anxiety holding me back for so long, but that's the kind of thing we tell ourselves to explain our lack of success. During some soul searching after my aunt died, I realized I have a fear of failure, but, worse, I also had a fear of <u>success</u>. I would succeed a little, then fall right back because it scared me to think that I might actually have to pull my finger out and take action. I didn't know what to do next—how to scale my business or even if I wanted to.

After so much frustration and hating the cold climate where I was living, I made the choice to move again. I got my aunt's unit ready for sale and sold it on the first open day. I moved to Queensland, the sunshine state.

I have now been here on my little island for nine months, and I am loving life. I am finally reaping the rewards of never giving up and learning the skills needed to succeed.

I finally have worked out some of that Rubik's Cube and can't wait to solve more.

## BIOGRAPHY

Karyn Mahoney is an Aussiepreneur Action Coach and a founder of YEP—Young Entrepreneur Project. Karyn is passionate about helping others achieve their dreams. She has been involved in network marketing and direct selling for over twenty years. Karyn achieved No. 1 New Manager in sales for Australia and New Zealand in 2016 and still holds the record for most sold in one week in her distributorship—more than

$14K. Karyn also ran a successful AIRBNB Cleaning business on the Mornington Peninsula, Victoria, Australia. Karyn's vision is to bring knowledge and training with massive action guidance to Aussie business owners, so they can also be successful Aussiepreneurs. Karyn also loves dogs and has fostered many over the years, which her own dog, Koda, loves to help out with. Karyn also helps out raising funds and volunteering for the community and kids on the small Island in Queensland, Australia, where she lives as a caregiver for her uncle.

Contact Karyn Mahoney via https://linktr.ee/KarynMahoney

## CHAPTER 21

# The Deeper Why

*By Leah Clout*

I was about nine when I was honest with my mum for the first time about how I felt about my self-belief and appearance. I sat across from her and told her how much I hated looking in the mirror. "I don't want to be me anymore," I said. I will always remember the look of absolute horror on her face. She wasn't aware I had been facing extreme bullying, based on my appearance. Both my parents were supportive and loving, and they tried to help me in every way possible. But from that young age, I felt as though my sparkle had disappeared. I was convinced I would never be good enough as I was, not for anything.

Throughout my teens, I continued settling for being average, sometimes below average. That was me, hiding away in the toilets at college to avoid social situations, getting into bad relationships. And as much as my parents assured me I was fantastic, that I was good enough, I never believed it myself. I vividly remember, aged thirteen, walking home from the local park one day with shards of glass stuck in my cardigan after having had a bottle thrown at me, all the while being taunted that I was too ugly to be wearing it. Those kids acted as though I was not worthy of having nice things, and they intentionally spoiled it for me. And still, I said nothing. I accepted that kind of treatment because I believed I deserved no better. I carried on with my life, saying nothing.

That feeling continued for many years. I had my first child in 2012, as a single parent, and I had a burning desire to give my daughter courage, confidence, and empower her to do more in life than I had. Despite this, I felt undeserving. In 2016, I was fortunate enough to marry an incredibly supportive man, the first and only person I can really be honest with. I wish I could see myself as he does! I was happy, and I had retrained into a new profession. I had far more than I believed I deserved.

In 2017, our second daughter was born, and I experienced a very traumatic birth. I recall saying goodbye to my husband as I was taken to an intensive care unit and honestly not believing I would see him again. As you can imagine, this had a severe effect on me; my bond with my second beautiful daughter was strong, but I was not strong at all. I knew I needed to focus my mind. I remember lying awake feeding my youngest and deciding I was going to be somebody. My family deserved more than I had been giving.

I joined the network marketing profession in 2018 with absolutely no experience. I was just a mum who wanted a better life; I had finally decided I would leave a legacy for my children—I was worthy! I looked into my children's eyes, and I realized I could only support them in becoming strong and successful women if I led by example. It was almost as if I started to sparkle again, for the first time in over eight years. The question was, how was I going to reach that confident place within myself?

For almost three years now, I have experienced the highs and lows of network marketing. I have made lots of mistakes. In my early days, I struggled to reach out to people for fear of rejection. I have even cried before going live because I was afraid someone would laugh at my appearance. But I wiped away those tears, popped a few notes around my screen to keep me focused, and I got back up again.

During my first eighteen months in this industry, I searched for my "Why." Was it to make a profit? Or buy a house and escape paying rent?

When I finally achieved both those goals, I realized success has nothing to do with material possessions. Of course, I was thrilled that my husband and I were now homeowners, but that was not my burning desire. My "Why" was buried much deeper than I had ever admitted to anyone, but when I finally established what it was, I blossomed.

I remember the first time I stood at the front of a room full of people and delivered a training slot; my hands were shaking, and I was terrified. Momentarily, I went back to my childhood and being taunted and pushed around. Once more, I felt that feeling of worthlessness, not being good enough to be standing up there in front of everyone. Then, magically, I was able to picture my mum's face on the day when I first told her, "I don't want to be me anymore."

I will never be that child again. I will never be that person again, nor will I ever allow my children to perceive me as that person. I am determined to be a positive influence in their lives! I can now fully imagine the heartbreak my mum must have felt hearing my words. As a mother myself, it flipped my switch! But that experience gives me the strength to get back up again each time life gets tough. In times like these, when COVID-19 has kept us apart from our loved ones, or times when I have to make a tough business decision, I think of that moment. I think of myself, my children, and of the thousands of young people today experiencing the same lack of self-worth I felt. I do it for them!

But while I had completely changed my mindset and was passionate about what I did, I kept hitting the "glass ceiling." I could not understand what I had to do to enable me to continue progressing and helping others.

I persevered, telling myself to:

Keep going
Keep going
Listen, learn, try again
Believe in yourself and keep going

Perseverance has been a crucial part of my personal development; the more I learned, the more I succeeded. And the more I learned about myself, the more I sparkled, which led to me delivering more trainings. Every time I went live or stood up and spoke to people, I felt better, and my confidence grew, so I performed better.

People began approaching me; I no longer had to chase them! People wanted to speak to me, and those people will never know how truly grateful I am to them. When I attended my first conference, I was called "inspirational" by people I had previously only ever communicated with online. What an incredible lift that gave me! But would I have felt that way if I had not put myself "out there" and braved the big wide world of network marketing?

In February 2020, I won an award within my company for team sales, and I ended up on stage to receive it wearing no shoes because I had kicked them off for comfort, having no clue I was about to be called up. But instead of being shy and feeling undeserving, I let myself be thrilled!

Having experienced both a state of having absolutely no self-belief and of complete euphoria and pride, I wouldn't wish my experience of self-doubt on anybody. I want to help others overcome their self-doubt and sparkle as they deserve. And just when I believed my passion was at its peak, business suddenly boomed, and I finally produced leaders within my business, five of them, all people I had helped. There was never a better feeling because when you think about what success really means, money has no place, belongings have no place. If you are unhappy, you cannot be truly successful. If you are not making a change in the world, what are you doing in other people's worlds? What will you pass on to those dearest to you?

Unfortunately, only a few short months after the business enjoyed a period of huge success, my eldest daughter came to me saying those familiar words, almost the exact same words I had said to my mum all that time ago. My beautiful bright girl said she didn't like looking in the mirror because she didn't like what she saw there.

How could this be happening? Had I failed as a parent? Had I failed in my goal as an advocate for confidence?

Absolutely not. I wanted to burst into tears, but I held her tight. I looked at my mum, who was there too, and for the very first time, I said to my children:

"I once felt that way too, but I don't anymore," and as I hugged her and listened to what she had to say, I realized I had a story to tell. I had the experience that, had I passed it on, might have helped prevent this outcome. But I could still support and guide her. I decided we should go live online; I would show her my world and that she can find success in life, too. I wanted her to understand she can become whatever she desires to be.

My daughter was interested in how I had changed the way I felt. We will continue to thrive and share this story so that other people can see there is light at the end of a dark place and that we all have a deeper purpose in life to be discovered.

When teaching you something, people often encourage you by saying, "If I can do this, you can too." This chapter is my next step in building my confidence and being a leader. I want to use my experience to create optimal confidence in the world, to inspire others to speak up and find their WHY.

My advice is to keep going, feel that drive and determination as you inhale, and push away the negative thoughts when you exhale.

Get back up again.

## BIOGRAPHY

Leah Clout is a successful leader in network marketing, helping people from all walks of life achieve their goals. Her mission is to be the best version of herself for her family and inspire others to live a life of optimal confidence. Leah is also known for her charitable work and determination to make a difference in the world.

Contact Leah Clout at https://linktr.ee/LeahClout

CHAPTER 22

# Use The Gifts You've Received In Life!

*By Leif Näsberg*

I woke up one day in February 2012 with a stomachache that lasted all morning, which didn't go away but kept coming back, and I couldn't help but ask myself why. This happened just as I had finally started to feel mentally well after having spent almost a year as part of a personal development group. We looked inward within ourselves with tools such as the power of thought, visualization, intuition, healing, and meditation. The members of the group opened up to each other in a way I had never experienced before. For the first time in my forty-seven years, I felt I had really invested in myself. I had been given tools I could use to understand myself and the environment.

**Listen to Your Gut Feeling**

I first joined the group because, about a year and a half earlier, I had involuntarily entered a new phase in life. I had been fired after fourteen years in my job due to "lack of work" following a company restructuring. At the same time, my cohabiting relationship ended after four years. We had met at a party, and when she stepped into the room, I was hit by lightning, and sweet music arose when we discovered how many things we shared in common. A few months down the line, I was convinced I'd met my life partner, even though things seemed a bit awkward at times. I finally understood why after two years, when she dared to tell me about another man in another country, whom she had left just before she met me. I thought our love grew stronger despite that, but after a retreat weekend session a year and a half later, crying and upset, she told me she realized her feelings for the man had returned. I spontaneously realized she must be able to find out what her real feelings were. So, a few weeks later, she went to see him, then came home, and confirmed the way she felt about him. We went our separate ways, and my heart was broken again. But at least this time, I had a reasonable explanation for what happened between us, unlike the ending of my marriage seven years earlier.

Luckily, I had a new job to focus on. After a month or so there, I spoke to a man with a sign about healing on his desk and asked some cautious questions about it. He gave me the information and, although I was skeptical, I signed up for a weekend course and tested group meditation. It felt like something I needed to explore further, so I took the course in personal development.

Remember, at that time, I was not feeling physically well. I brought it up in the group and got several suggestions about where I could turn for help. The group's coach also asked me to create a clear goal of how I would look and feel when I had reached the stage I wanted. The big pictures and feelings took shape, but the clearest goal that emerged was to change my waist measurement from wide (⊠) waist to narrow (v)—symbolized in Swedish by the letter V, meaning weight, wellness, winner.

So, I embarked on a diet and exercise program with a local organization and began to ditch all my old values about dieting, which involved using diet powders. After the introductory talk, I realized the more I had exercised, the more food I had eaten. My training coach and I set up an initial 12-week goal aimed at my losing 17 kilograms, with the help of their low-calorie diet, circuit training several times a week, walking at least 10,000 steps per day, and participating in group meetings. During the first three "kickstart" weeks, I ate only 600 calories per day, then 800, and, after three months, I made a slow return to a normal but healthier diet. I don't know where my focus to achieve my goal came from, but I reached it after just nine weeks, losing those 17 kilograms, reducing my waist by 18 cm, and my BMI by six units. My health coach and I were both amazed at the result. I had turned down invitations to barbecue parties and the like, but it was worth it because now I felt more self-secure, stronger, and sexier.

On this health journey, I had discovered a problem, sought help, changed old attitudes, focused, and acted. I had transformed my negative self-image into a positive one. The saying "To get something you never had; you have to do something you've never done" fits nicely in my case.

**Take advantage of your gifts**

The previous year, in my new job in the financial industry, I had had to take a test to obtain a license to stay in my position. I had heard many horror stories about how difficult the test was and how many people had failed it several times. Since I had no financial background, I was terrified and immediately envisioned myself failing. I knew I would have to work extremely hard and smart to succeed. It was like learning a whole new language in a very short time. The test consisted of five parts where I needed to score fifty percent each and at least seventy percent overall. My biggest asset was my understanding of law and ethics, but I knew my big stumbling block would be the math part. I made sure I learned everything about the former but realized I would have to pass on some of the most difficult math formulas during the test because they would stress me out too much. Besides, I didn´t need them for my role. So, I learned about the different contexts in which different formulas were used and some necessary calculations. I studied hard, and two days before the test, a clear picture suddenly appeared in my mind; it showed me slipping into the office and happily showing off my license. So, how did I do? Well, I passed on the first try, then danced in the sun on the streets of Stockholm back to the office, where I still work.

## Accept yourself

I jumped over the gym bench and ran after the floorball ball when I heard a crash behind me. When I turned my head to look, I hit a suspended gymnastic boom. I was fourteen, and three weeks later, I suffered my first epileptic seizure. I tried to live like my friends, and all went well if the activities were relatively quiet. But with high school came dance parties, alcohol, and freedom. I became a DJ, got some small gigs, and began to broadcast on local radio. But I suffered from regular seizures, so I realized I couldn't live quite like a "normal" teenager. The illness prevented me from getting a driver's license and doing military service, important milestones on the journey from boy to man. The limitations made me feel uncertain of my own masculinity for a few years.

I have now had ten years free of seizures. The disease has clearly affected and limited me during my life in many ways, but I have worked gradually to lessen its impact. My main method for successfully doing so has been acceptance: "Accepting others is great, accepting oneself is greatest."—Leif Näsberg

## Losses and sorrows

Those limitations and, perhaps, a lack of experience probably affected me when choosing a wife. I met her at work, and we fell in love, but it was not as though lightning struck us. However, I was very much in love and felt proud when we got married. A few years later, we had a son, and everything changed. My family became the most important thing in my life, but my wife became completely focused on our son. I slowly but surely became less important in her life. I suffered increasingly because of our emotionless relationship, where all closeness gradually disappeared. On several occasions, I suggested we attend couples therapy, which she refused. I then developed a form of depression, comfort ate, and slept for several hours during the middle of the day on the weekends. I also got acid reflux and vomited bile in the mornings.

One day, I found myself sitting in front of the railroad tracks thinking about ending my life, which I realized was a cowardly way out. At home, the way my wife and I communicated had started to negatively affect our son, and I knew we had to get a divorce. Once I moved out, I fought hard to get joint custody of our son, but my ex-wife opposed it, even though we had initially agreed to it. Naively, I complied. Luckily, my son and I were able to meet regularly, but I didn`t have any involvement in his everyday life. After six months, my son told me he thought I'd done the right thing by moving out because I seemed much happier than before. I felt he was right, and the previous ailments I had suffered from during the marriage ceased after a few months. The divorce and its aftermath have been the cause of my biggest sense of loss and grief in life so far. Aged eighteen, following the effects of my accident, my male self-image had been badly shaken. Now, I had also lost the positive image of myself as a husband and family provider. However, I had no choice but to divorce my wife to feel good about myself again. The insight I gained is that only you can influence your own happiness.

**Inspiration and preparation**

"It was an inspiring story, so I will buy your book when it comes out," I told the woman sitting next to me at the table. She had been telling me about the book she had written about her pilgrimage from Camino Frances to Santiago de Compostela. After listening to her, I felt I would like to do that hike at some point. A year and a half later, in September 2015, I was ready. I had prepared well and trained to 250 km, but, despite that, I had also built up in my mind horrible scenarios of loneliness, delusion, and giving up. The first day's hike followed the tough climbs of the Pyrenees and took between eight and nine hours to complete. After a few days, I met Simon, and we started hiking together, got parted, then reunited again along the way. We became a close-knit team and supported each other. After twenty-five days, we had walked the 800km to Santiago de Compostela. It was a fantastic experience, allowing me to leave all concerns about everyday life behind, which gave me a tremendous sense of inner peace. The following year, I hiked another, shorter route; the Camino Portuguese.

**Stupidity & important lessons**

I was unprepared when, in the spring of 2019, I hiked the Camino Norte, the longest and hardest road. I envisioned myself doing it but walked for much longer stretches than I could handle. After ten days, I became ill and went to the hospital, where I was diagnosed with pneumonia. After a week in a Spanish hospital, with oxygen and strong medicines, I went home to Sweden. The rehabilitation took a few months, and the symptoms, remarkably like COVID-19, lasted for about a year. That trip was a hard lesson, one I hope I have learned a lot from, something I acknowledge by writing these words.

**Never quit following your dreams**

I have a dream of doing more to help others and have a freer, richer, and more loving life for myself. This dream has led me to take coaching courses and getting involved in network marketing. I haven't yet worked as a professional coach, but I have used the skills I have acquired on myself and others with some success. As early as 2009, I took my first steps in network marketing. Without great commitment and, therefore, little success, I have so far been part of three different companies. The products and services have been incredibly good for me, and I have also made lots of good, close friends at the latest company I've joined. It was recently bought by another company. Now I have finally gotten deeply involved. With some real effort, it is paying off. I recently received my first income from network marketing.

## BIOGRAPHY

Leif Näsberg is an ordinary Swedish man but, at the same time, unique. He has a positive outlook on life and is a genuinely kind and humble man. He loves dance, deep conversations, and personal development. Leif has extensive experience in service, customer care, and problem-solving, having worked for fourteen years handling sales and customer complaints. His sense of service developed early on in the professional grocery industry, with sales of fresh food. He has now been working in the financial industry for ten years. His curiosity led him to participate in several courses in personal development, such as ICF coaching, spiritual healing, and WOWX leadership training. Also, he has walked the pilgrim routes to Santiago de Compostela three times. Bringing out and using your gifts is his underlying message.

Contact Leif Näsberg via https://linktr.ee/Leif_Nasberg

CHAPTER 23

# Box? What Box?

*By Lori Ryan*

Parents are taught that the most important job they have when raising children is to instill a sense of right and wrong: morals and principles that guide our behaviors, decisions, actions, and values. As children, we begin to live our lives in accordance with these teachings. In essence, these morals and values define who we are and guide how we interpret the world around us. These beliefs become very strong parameters that also determine our perception of success, worth, and wealth. Let's say that these parameters make up the sides of a box.

As we get older and have our own experiences, we can think in one of two ways. First, we can continue to limit our thoughts based on what's contained inside this box, always conforming and never rocking the boat. Good ideas come from inside-the-box thinking. Second, we can think outside the box to develop more creative, unusual ideas, separate from the rules and limitations contained within the box. Great ideas come from outside-the-box thinking. What if there was another way of thinking? What if we got up every day, making decisions, choices, and goals based on thinking that there was NO box? Our ideas would be limitless. Just imagine that freedom! A clean slate. The possibilities would be endless. No assumptions. No constraints. No biases. Everything we thought impossible would become possible. Radical, right? Not really. Lots of people are already doing this. I just didn't know I could be one of them because my mode of thinking was holding me back.

We have all heard, "We become what we think." Truer words have never been spoken. Without even realizing it, this becomes a mantra for many of us. Case in point, it was only recently that I was talking to a team member about setting goals. She told me that she didn't need to climb up to a higher position in her job because she didn't need to earn that much money, to which she added, 'I wasn't raised that way,' almost as if her birthright was determining her future and measure of worth and success. Abundance, especially an abundance of money, was not something she was comfortable with. Not only was she not comfortable with it, but she perceived it as something negative. Her thoughts were bound by the limitations contained in the box she had been carrying around since her childhood.

Abundance is defined as "more than enough; a lot of." Most of us can talk freely and openly about the abundance of love, trust, wildlife, rainfall, food, and various other things. Still, we get very uncomfortable talking about the abundance of wealth. Why? What makes having more than enough money a bad thing? What if we shifted our mindset to see an abundance of wealth as not just being about money but options? Options to choose when we worked, who we worked with, and how much money we made; options to spend more time with our kids, our partners, our friends, our pets, and yes, even ourselves. In order to have those options, we need money.

I wanted to have these options my entire life. I wanted freedom of time. So, why not me? Let's rewind to my childhood. I was raised Catholic in a small town in Newfoundland and Labrador, Canada, and the teaching that defined my way of thinking was, "One cannot serve both God and money." I was raised to perceive abundance as wasteful. Amassing great wealth was for greedy, materialistic people, and show-offs. An abundance of wealth was just not on the top of my list of things to accomplish in life. My list included daily prayers, confession, and sacrifice. Don't get me wrong. I had a very comfortable life. I was raised by a very strong, educated woman. I never wanted for anything. But even as a young girl, I knew I didn't want to do what everyone else was doing. But I lacked direction. I lacked the ability to think without limitations—to think as if there was no box.

I needed to rewire the way I was thinking. I needed to wholeheartedly step away from the mentality that "making ends meet" was an acceptable goal—the mentality that I should be satisfied with average. I needed to embrace the thought that wanting abundance was not something to feel ashamed of or guilty about, that I wasn't being selfish for wanting options or for wanting to be more than average. So, what did I have to do? Where did I have to start? I had no idea. Believe me, changing my way of thinking would take a while.

When I finished high school, I left my hometown to experience the world, with a suitcase full of clothes and a wallet void of cash. Let me tell you, I soon learned the world was an expensive place. I loved traveling and all the crazy, cool experiences that came along with it. But I hated every job I needed to hold down in order to make just enough money to buy my next plane ticket. I supported myself like that for several years, where amassing "just enough" was my goal. Work, save, spend. Work, save, spend. Wash, rinse, repeat.

Even after finishing my second degree in university, I was making choices out of fear and lack, not out of abundance. Oh, except for the abundance of student loan debt I had amassed (also not easy to talk about). But again, I had no motivation to make more than I needed because I never measured my success in terms of money. I had become an average adult on a payment plan, not because I couldn't be greater than average, but because average was easier and safer.

You see, no one messes with average. Average is supported. I'm not a psychologist or a self-help expert, but I am a woman who has conformed for many years, not because it was the most comfortable place for me to be, but because it was easier and safer. For me, being average was the opposite of comfortable. You know the saying, "Square peg in a round hole?" That was me. I always felt like I didn't quite fit into the conventional mold. I never thought or acted unconventionally, or if I did, it didn't last long enough to take hold in my thoughts, and therefore, my actions.

Like most people, I have spent my adult life trading my time for money to make ends meet. Fast forward a number of years: I was now a single mom working long hours as an independent consultant to support my two children. My success came at a heavy price. I always felt like I was too busy, keeping the wheels on the bus turning, to enjoy the journey. I would look back on previous years with guilt, wishing I had been more present to my kids. I was selling my soul to make ends meet in a stressful, thankless job for most of my adult life. I was unhappy, angry at myself for not "trying" harder, stressed to the max, and always wishing and hoping for a way out and more time. I still longed for freedom of time. Even when I tried to talk about my feelings of unhappiness and unfulfillment to others in my inner circle, they would all say, 'We get it. We are all in the same boat.' But I wanted off that boat. I wanted abundance. I was now starting to understand that wishing and hoping were never going to help me manifest it.

It has taken me a long time to realize my thoughts were defining me, that I had become what I was always thinking. Headed towards the second half of my life, I knew it was time to change my mantra.

In order to make that happen, I first had to change my thinking. I had to imagine that I could have everything I wanted and more—that I deserved it and that it wasn't wrong of me to want abundance. I didn't have to let go of my past. But I had to take everything I had learned over the years, my failures, successes, and everything contained within the box I've been carrying with me my entire life, and learn to pivot. To change my thinking would ultimately change my direction.

Second, I had to stop imagining and truly believe that the impossible was possible. That I could determine my path, my journey. I had to shift my mindset to truly believe that I was not just capable but unstoppable. I had to believe, that with the right thoughts, my beliefs could become my reality.

Finally, I needed to take action. The saying goes, "Necessity is the mother of invention." What if necessity was the mother of reinvention? Not only was I in need, but I now understood what I needed. It was time for me to reinvent, rebrand, and rethink. I began to think as if there was no box. This didn't mean I undid everything my parents taught me. For example, knowing right from wrong is not a bad thing. It just meant that I evolved from what they taught me so I could reach higher goals, a higher potential. When I shifted my thoughts, I was able to see clearer, go outside my comfort zone, envision a better future, and achieve goals I never thought possible.

I believe we are all destined for our sense of greatness, and achieving that greatness is always a work in progress. I continue to learn on my journey, and I know that I am not done yet. In many ways, I feel that I have only just begun to live my life authentically.

None of you reading this book are average. You all have the ability to think like there is no box—to manifest abundance with the right thought processes. The only thing holding you back is you. Be brave. Be courageous. Be your own superhero. Take the first step, and I promise that every step forward after that will get easier and easier.

I will end with this. How do you want to be remembered? What do you want on your obituary? I know I don't want mine to say, "Lori was an average, hard-working lady. She will be missed." I want it to say, "Lori was a trailblazer who lived her life to the fullest, who picked herself up when she fell, and who always did it her way. Her legend lives on."

Go on. Be a legend in your mind and change the world!

## BIOGRAPHY

Lori Ryan is an independent consultant based in Calgary, Alberta. She implements technology, people, and business process changes for large-scale transformational projects for multiple industries. She has completed her master's in International Development, has a post-grad degree in Information Technology, and holds a Project Management Professional designation. As a business leader, Lori thrives on brainstorming sessions, crazy ideas, laughing out loud, and building high-performing teams. Lori has recently entered the Network Marketing industry, where she uses her leadership skills to hit the leader boards and guide her team to achieve their full potential. When Lori is not working, she can be found planning her next adventure with her children and their rescue dog.

Contact Lori Ryan via https://linktr.ee/Lori_Ryan

CHAPTER 24

# Born For Greatness

*By Martine Viney*

Significance is one of the six core needs. My life was built around it. I was born in Mauritius, a little island in the Indian Ocean, into a hardworking family. I wanted everything I did not have. I wanted to have white skin, be number one in sports, have a life like those on TV, and be beautiful. But I was just average.

One great thing that worked for me, though, was my mindset. Of course, I did not know that it was a "thing" at the time. I realize now that I used to have "screenshots," like computer snippets, that lasted only a split second. I think at first it was completely unconscious, but then I realized that they were coming true. I learned to recognize them. I knew the emotional connection to that "thing" at that second was what created what I wanted, years before learning "The Secret."

My determination for significance drove my life, gave it a purpose; it was like a hunger. It was not to be found elsewhere within my family and friends. I was very average in everything I did. The perception of myself at the time was "normal," even below average. Others had "it," but I did not. Family members made sure I realized I was average, or was it just my perception at the time? I had the drive; I was determined to be different; big, smart, and beautiful. I wanted to prove to all of "Them" that I was extraordinary.

At seven years of age, I had a particular screenshot go off in my brain; while at the airport to pick up my uncle, it came to me that I would live in Australia. And, in 1996, I emigrated to Australia to study. I had the certainty that it was my place. I graduated twice, and I became a chartered accountant. Finally, I realized that education was my Significance. I could show it to everyone, and I was very good at it. I had a system to get it done: Hard work, arduous work, and no play!

Screenshot of a fully-written diary; for me, that meant business, important meetings; Significance. I got things done and got promoted repeatedly. I did have a busy life, being married with two kids, and a full-on career. I pushed everything else aside, including myself, having decided that nothing and no-one would get in my way. I got divorced, bought my first home, and two investment properties by myself. I remember being in bed with my younger son taking calls about bidding on a property! I surely did not know what I was doing, but I won it. I knew I would; I had the certainty.

I trusted the Universe entirely, and it responded in abundance all the time. I made swift decisions, although I often scared myself. It brought a sense of Significance and pride in me from my parents. At last, I knew I was special, above average. Then, I bought a car, took my boys swimming on the Great Barrier Reef when they were five- and six-years-old, and spent ten days at Sea World Resort with them. More Significance.

Screenshot again; I would be a millionaire. So, I read *The Secret*, finally. I studied it, wrote the points down, and practiced. It worked. Before long, I had reached above one million dollars in assets. But around the age of thirty-five, I started to feel an unease inside, a pressure, a heaviness. Doubt crept into that well-oiled machine. What if the system stopped working for me? What if I could not maintain my lifestyle anymore? All that I had built up could be snatched away at any time. I was sure that people were waiting for me to fail; "They" wanted what I had, "They" were coming for me. Or, more likely, I was waiting for me to fail. I had started questioning the power of the Universe, and it responded.

I felt like there was nothing for me to achieve anymore. I was done. I went into protection mode, guarding what was dear to me; my job, my belongings, my children. I decided to play it low, play it small, be among the crowd. Suddenly, being the norm, average was what I wanted.

Slowly, things got taken away: My bosses turned out to be arrogant pricks; I smashed up my beautiful car twice; I had no job satisfaction, I was not paid enough. It seemed the world was demanding more from me than I had to give. I ran away when it became too hard, when "They" wanted too much, hiding behind locked doors, under the covers. I only dared come out to earn a living and for the kids to finish school. The plan was to sell all my investments and retire with a couple of million. I wanted to disappear, and playing small was my priority. I wondered, is this depression?

When I got married a second time, to Gerry, a man I love and who still loves me, I moved further into "average." Now, he was there to rescue me, protect me, save me from all of "Them" who were waiting for me to fail. I played housewife. My obsession was having a perfect, clean house. I played trophy wife when I accompanied him on his business trips. I played the perfect mother when the kids were back from school.

Gerry gave me everything I ever wanted, but unhappiness was coming out of my pores, almost choking me. But I had no reason to be unhappy. I told myself, there are millions of people who want the life I have. Being grateful was easily said and done at the time; in fact, I felt guilty. I had nothing to justify being unhappy, so I had to play my role. My son, who is on the autism spectrum, became that reason. Yep, people got it and related to my pain as a mother of an autistic child. It feels dreadful writing that, but it was the truth. So, I stuck with it for a long time, until he smacked me on the face one day while on holiday.

I fell flat on my face, literally. He had a big meltdown, and I was the one creating it, so he slapped me. Suddenly, I felt lost, scared, depressed, fearful of the next move to be made. I knew I had to change and that I still had it in me, but I could not reach it. I did not know where to start, or if it was even possible to get out of the hole that I had dug so deep.

Screenshot: The world does not owe you anything. Something happened when my son hit me; the world did not stop to check how I was doing. He moved on, the family moved on fairly quickly, as we were visiting Philadelphia. But I was stuck in that moment, realizing it was not just about being hit by my son during a meltdown but also the Universe waking me up, telling me that it does not owe me anything; my future is for me to decide. Did I want to turn the situation around? I had a choice.

Something had to change. Average was not what I had ever wanted to be. No-one was going to rescue me or save me; I had complete control of my life. I had done it before, and I knew I could do it again. And I promised myself, this time it will be on my terms, it will be for me alone; I had to work on myself.

Screenshot: What you focus on you create. The lump in my throat took a while to go. I worked on myself one day at a time. I openly shared my emotions with my family; they needed to see what I was hiding inside and why. None of it made sense but saying it out loud helped.

I wanted a life of abundance and fulfillment, so I worked on my limiting beliefs and replaced them one by one. I increased my level of awareness around my self-talk. I consciously questioned the feelings I had in different circumstances and became immensely curious about my thoughts. I chose the right people to hang out with. I learned to say 'no' more often.

I believe in education, so I learned about coaching. This education was for me, for my soul. I checked the recurring themes, the patterns that had occurred throughout my life. Making money is what I am good at. Professionally, I felt I had reached a glass ceiling until I realized that I could break through it—there was another level I could tap into, another world I did not know existed, or that I could be a part of.

I choose to believe that I visualize what I want, connect with it emotionally, as if it has already happened, and my subconscious mind finds ways to make it happen. I choose to believe there are enough resources for all of us to have whatever we need or want; you just need to tap into it, take what you need—it is unlimited— you do not need to pay it back.

I choose to believe that wealth creation is what drives me, so I can take care of everyone around me, like my community, and by providing this education to immigrants and refugees. I choose to believe that my purpose in life is to educate others that they have everything to create the life they have been dreaming of. I choose to believe it is my mission to be fully me, with my past in the present and in the future. I choose to believe that I am the master of my Universe.

Our minds create what we focus on. You truly have the ability to create anything you want in your life. Once the focus is set, your mind finds ways to make it happen for you. This happens to all of us, not just the rich and famous, but all of us around the world, no matter our circumstances, situation, or special conditions.

Once you get that, then you start to meet the right people, you see opportunities and success come in through the open door. Visualize and take action. Take massive action, as Tony Robbins would say. Model yourself on people who have done it before you; learn about their successes and replicate them. You are the driver of your bus-of-life, no-one else. The world does not owe you anything. It is all up to you.

Build a system that you can use when you get low. I have a Harry Potter wand on my desk. When I hear my inner voice sending fear signals to my brain, I stand up, do a Super Woman pose (hand on the hips) with my Harry Potter wand and, just like magic, the stick works. I believe it works for me; it chases the negative thoughts away. I share my office with my husband, and it does make him laugh, but he understands all of me. Find something that will work for you, a go-to you can use when your emotions are low, or before a meeting, an interview, or some event that you will remember.

Believe that change is instantaneous. You can switch from sad to happy, from frustration to focus, from anger to gratefulness in seconds. Make decisions regularly, especially those that move you towards your ultimate purpose. Make decisions quickly, fail forward, and learn from them. On your deathbed, it will be the decisions that you did not take you will remember.

Be curious about yourself and others, about life, about the world; ask lots of questions. Always be prepared to learn from anyone, from any level, regarding anything. Come with an open mind to conversations, listen more, talk less, take it in; you could be changing your life or, more importantly, affecting someone else's life positively. Give Significance to others who deserve it and be humble while you create greatness. Work hard, push through the tough stuff until you reach the other side, where you can enjoy the fruits of your efforts.

Laser-focus your mind on your purpose every day.

Be certain that you are born to achieve greatness.

## BIOGRAPHY

Martine Viney is a chartered accountant and business coach who specializes in turning average businesses into successful businesses. She owns CoachMe Institute, a coaching business providing education and programs to future leaders and rainmakers. She is currently the secretary on the board of a non-profit organization whose mission is education. Her passion is to share knowledge, especially to individuals who need it most, teaching them that change is possible, that their duty is to create the life of their dreams and impact the world. Martine is a wife, mother, and stepmother to five children. She currently resides in Melbourne, Australia.

Contact Martine Viney via https://linktr.ee/martineviney

CHAPTER 25

# Searching For The Smartest Way To Make A Good Life

*By Morten Andersen*

I had been waiting for the message. I had looked forward to this day for a year. I looked at the CEO and said, "Thank you," and hurried back to my office. Sat down, closed my eyes, and started to cry.

Why did I feel like that? After all, it's what I wanted. Why am I so sad? Why do I feel this overwhelming sense of loss?

It was my life, my top priority, and my identity—I had spent all my time and energy on it for eight years. And now, it's over. I packed a few things and left the office. None of my eighty-five employees knew yet. It was the last time I saw most of them.

At home, I told my wife what had happened. She warmly hugged and congratulated me. That's when I first noticed the feeling of freedom. It was barely noticeable in the sea of sadness, confusion, and fear, but it was there.

Fourteen years earlier, when graduating from engineering school, I started my first job as a software and hardware developer in a husband-and-wife company. Being their first employee, it was the closest to being an entrepreneur myself. As the company grew, I engaged in all kinds of work: project management, sales, customer support, delivering training courses, and production, in addition to my main job developing software and hardware. What a great way to learn!

This was also when I was first introduced to network marketing. I was blown away by the concept, and we started out as part-time network marketers. We never made it big in that company, but we learned a lot about sales and entrepreneurship.

I remained in my first job for five years. Being an employee, without a doubt, had its benefits: decent salary, interesting job, good colleagues, great business travels, and flexible working hours. There was nothing to complain about. Most of my colleagues from my previous jobs are still employees. For them, it's clearly the right thing.

For me, it was not. I wanted to create my future, not working for someone else. In 1991, I was ready. I knew that starting my own company was going to be hard work. It would be tough to live without a salary for weeks, or maybe months. I was totally fine with it!

I founded the company together with two friends, and our first office was the guest bedroom in my home. We developed advanced software for the telecom industry, obtained our first few customers, and six months later, we were able to move into a real office.

The first two years, we paid ourselves very little, often nothing, so we could employ more people, move to a bigger office, and grow. I worked at least eighty hours a week, and it was fun. It's incredible what is possible when running on pure ambition, enthusiasm, and the joy of creating something from nothing!

For me, it was all about freedom. My definition of freedom was not to avoid work; it was to create, to not have a boss telling me what I can and cannot do, and of course, to have the possibility of a very good income, much more than any regular job would ever pay.

But the freedom came with a price, and after three years, we had to give up our plan to grow without investors. Growth costs money, lots of money. Developing more products, increasing marketing activities, and selling more meant that we needed even bigger offices, more equipment, more inventory, and more employees.

With investors on board, we continued the growth. With eighty-five employees, we developed and sold expensive solutions to big telecom operators in twenty-five countries. When we were finally ready to enter the US market, we decided to partner with a company from Virginia. They needed what we had, and they ended up buying the company.

Moneywise, it was great. I got well paid for my share of the company. I had no problem signing for the one condition they had: the three founders would have to stay in the company for three years.

It turned out to be a big problem. After six years of hard work, with responsibility for numerous employees and customers, taking risks, and having had very little time off, I was tired. The enthusiasm I used to have was gone. The feeling of freedom I initially had was also gone. I had gone from being an enthusiastic, creative, free entrepreneur to a burnt-out employee.

Have you ever experienced a real burn-out? I mean, not temporarily being exhausted and needing a vacation, but being entirely stripped of energy and not finding any joy or enthusiasm for the things you do anymore. Everything becomes hard. You just want to quit, escape, sleep, and not talk to anyone.

I did my best to do a decent job as CTO of the company. I became pretty good at hiding what I truly felt and disciplining myself to do what I needed to do. And, of course, it only got worse. One day I just had to admit that this was it; I could not take it anymore. I told the CEO and asked the board to release me from the contract. It took over a year before they did.

Free. Finally. Burnt-out, but free. It took me a week to recover from the worst sadness and feeling of disappointment in myself. At the end of the week, the potential of a fresh start got more and more exciting, but I still did not know what I wanted, only what I did not want.

Should I go back to being a regular employee? In a way, it was tempting—a fixed salary every month, normal working hours, and no responsibility for the company. If something happened, I could just find myself another job. With my experience, I could have found a great, well-paying job.

Should I start a new company? If so, what would I do? What kind of business? And most importantly, how would I avoid what put me in this situation?

My friends told me to get a regular job. After all, that's what *they* did. The more I thought about having a job, the clearer it became. I'm an entrepreneur. I have tasted the feeling of freedom, and I want it again.

So, I decided to give the dream another chance, and this time it should be different. I decided that no matter what kind of business I started, it had to fulfill my no-negotiable requirements:

1. No employees, no expensive offices, or other big overhead costs
2. No external investors, requiring very little capital for growth
3. Very high-income potential
4. No opening hours or fixed working hours
5. Interesting work where I can express myself, use my creativity, learn, and grow
6. Must be meaningful to me and to my clients/customers; something of which I will be proud

I don't mind working hard, as long as I do it with enthusiasm and freedom. Then it's not really work; it's a lifestyle of contribution, growth, and expression.

I believe what we get is what we focus on. I was so obsessed with finding the right business idea that I know what happened next was no coincidence. I saw an ad in *Entrepreneur Magazine* for a "Small Business Expo" in Dallas. Living in Norway, Dallas was far away, but I felt I just had to go there. That's where I met the person that re-introduced me to network marketing.

I did have years of experience from network marketing as a side business, more like a hobby, but I had not considered it as a "real" business before. Looking at my list of requirements and what a serious network marketing business in a good company would be like, I understood that this probably was exactly what I had been looking for.

We went all in. We started with the clear intention and goal of going *to the top* of our chosen company. This was not going to be a "try and see" thing like we had treated our previous network marketing side business.

We decided to work as professionals from day one. After many years as an employee and running my own company, I had no problems treating this as a professional business the same way. One of my goals was time-freedom with no fixed working hours. But that do not mean *no* working hours; it means deciding your own working hours.

I knew that going to the top requires that we learn from those already at the top, from the best. It's like when I decided to become an engineer, I did not learn to become a professional software and hardware developer from a random friend. I did not think that I was better than my teachers at engineering school. Of course not. I learned from the best, and gradually became a great engineer.

I applied the same principle in my network marketing business. I listened to my sponsor and mentors, took their advice, did the activities, and it worked.

I remember they told me there will be challenges like in any other business, and to reach the top, you must accept that challenges are a part of the business, and life. Going to the top, building a great business means working through the challenges and leveraging them to learn, grow and become stronger. Not understanding this is why most people in network marketing fail and ultimately quit.

Treating the business as a business paid off, and we reached the company's top position in less than four years. With that came several recognitions such as "Distributor of the Year" more than once, becoming members of the millionaire's club, and other cool perks.

But most importantly, I had created a business that fulfilled everything on my list, i.e., all my no-negotiables! I got the life I wanted, a life of freedom. I could work from home and be home when the kids came back from school. I could go on a three-week vacation whenever I wanted, without having to ask for time off.

The feeling of doing something important was also an essential factor; changing the lives of thousands for the better by helping others start their own businesses and experience the amazing benefits of the products!

The contrast to the life I had in my previous business and as an employee was huge!

It was about thirty-five years ago I started my first network marketing side business, and I have been a full-time network marketer for over twenty years now. I have also funded and been involved in a few new "traditional" companies over those years, all made possible by the residual income and time freedom I got from network marketeing.

To me, network marketing has paved the way to business-freedom, life-freedom, and living up to my fullest potential. I'm an entrepreneur by heart; I like to create and build businesses. And the great thing about network marketing is that the building and growing never stops, unless you want it to. You can take it as far as you like; there are no upper limits.

The potential in network marketing is so immense that I decided to stop all activities with my other businesses a few years ago. Network marketing is all about helping others become the best they can be, regardless of the company they are associated with. It's a profession of service to others, making a change in the world, and creating more freedom.

Having been an employee and an employer, having had network marketing as a side business and a main business, I know what's right for me. I know I can help anyone who wants a fulfilling life and freedom to succeed. Network marketing is truly the best and the most fair business model for this century.

## BIOGRAPHY

Morten Andersen is a passionate entrepreneur and business coach. He started his career as an employee, developing software and hardware. He has been an employer of the three technology companies which he started. Morten has also built large, international businesses as a network marketer. With thirty-five years of extensive experience from all sides of business life, this book is vital for anyone that considers starting a business and dreams of a better life.

Morten has previously written two books about business. He's an experienced speaker and has been speaking at several business conferences in Europe, the USA, and China. And with his long experience as a successful network marketer, he is a sought-after trainer and mentor. He loves traveling, experiencing new countries, cultures, and food.

Contact Morten Andersen via http://www.mortenandersen.info

CHAPTER 26

# Thrive In Adversity

*By Patrice Maurer*

Thriving is an attitude, one like Nietzsche wrote about. What does not kill you makes you stronger.[22]

But if you were my friend and needed my advice to survive a life of tragedy that brought pain and suffering, this is NOT what you would want to hear. In fact, if I were to tell you "Never give up" and "Whatever you must face, it will be worth it," you would dismiss me from your home and possibly your life.

And you would be right to do so.

So, I will not give you hollow words or some dead philosopher's quote. Instead, may I share with you how I overcame one adversity after another and decided not just learning to survive but rather thrive in real-life adversity?

As a little boy, I just knew I had a great destiny. That I would somehow receive an important mission in life. I simply could not have imagined what I would have to face to overcome challenges along the way.

My mother and father were ordinary hard-working people. I came to understand that I arrived a little too soon. My mother stayed at home to educate my sister and me. My sister came along three years after I did,

---

22 "Friedrich Nietzsche Quotes," BrainyQuote (Xplore), accessed March 30, 2021, https://www.brainyquote.com/quotes/friedrich_nietzsche_101616.

followed by my brother four years later. My mother only went back to work when my brother was fourteen years old.

My father worked hard, worked overtime, built our house, made a career in the factory where he worked, and climbed the social ladder until his retirement. He is still enjoying his retirement today at over seventy-nine years of age. His example is my model of righteousness, rigor, and perseverance.

Life was grand, and our family was loving. We grew happily despite minor sibling disputes.

When I began nursery school, I spoke only the Alsatian dialect. Alsace is a region in eastern France, along the German border, where the dialect was still prevalent in the 1960s and 1970s. It is a dialect close to German (75% German, 25% French). But despite pressure from the French government after the Second World War, with the return of Alsace to France, they could not manage to make it disappear. So, by my time in elementary school, I was fluent in French.

My elementary teacher oddly noted on my report card that I was a dreamer. I remember the event very well because she scolded me with the same comment so often. It may have been this dreaming that attracted attention from bullies who would routinely beat me up. I never understood why. I just felt betrayed!

The bullying continued throughout secondary school, and I was not a fighter at all. So, I just endured the violence. Eventually, I became unstable, and my grades started to plummet. And even though math was my favorite subject in primary school, I lost interest in it, leading my father to scold me that I didn't work enough, that I dreamed too much, and that I played too much. He would make me feel inadequate by comparing me to children who had better grades and to my cousin. But it was true. My escape from life was my playtime. So, I played in secret.

This conflict continued. My father pushed me into math. But I hated it. What I loved was foreign to him. My passions included history, collecting rare coins, and I simply loved to read, devouring book after book.

And yes, I still dreamed a lot, despite all the scolding.

To escape, I searched for a solution. I got a job during college. There were no alternatives, and I had applied to the professional hotel school. If I had not been accepted there, there would have been no choice other than an apprenticeship.

For me, it was obvious; I would be accepted into hotel school. But my parents, always so scared and indecisive, passed their doubts and fears onto me. Looking back, I realize that generation functioned entirely from a place of self-doubt: a prison made of self-induced fear.

From this place, I learned to struggle with self-doubt. Becoming fragile from the constant bullying, I grew into a victim. The harassment reached its peak with bullies knocking me off my bike. Scratched and bewildered, I stood up. I faced the pack of laughing hyenas without so much as a flinch. On my way home, I wondered: is this my future?

Imagine my relief when I graduated from secondary. I felt it was a fresh start, one where bullies no longer existed. But this "beginning" would last for the next forty-five years! I was an insecure seventeen-year-old! I did not feel that I was moving towards my dream of becoming an important and recognized person. I wasn't popular, I didn't have the drive, and I hadn't chosen the easiest path. It was 1982: my first year at the hotel school.

After several false starts in the hospitality industry, I found a job in Germany at a gastronomic restaurant in Freiburg, Breisgau. A young French chef gave me my start. But from the beginning, I was frustrated that I was preparing delicacies for people who were enjoying life on the other side of the wall, whereas I was stuck in that kitchen.

I was determined to make a considerable change, so I joined the army! For the first eighteen months, I served as the bartender in the NCO's mess. But very quickly, I understood that this also was not what I was looking for.

After the army, I went to work in Basel, Switzerland, but returned to France, where I was hired at the restaurant for Peugeot's car factory executives in Mulhouse. There, I rebelled—the same scenario. I realized that I was *not* made to work in those environments. The same scenario would systematically repeat itself. My history of switching from one restaurant to another only displaced the problem from one place to the next. It was a carousel: same problem, different city.

I noticed the salespeople who sold products to the chefs I worked with. I dreamed of changing my life, and becoming a salesman seemed intriguing. So, after I applied, I was interviewed by a psychologist, who told me that I was unfit for the job.

I felt disappointment, but no sense of resignation!

Shortly afterwards, I discovered network marketing. I had my first clients and several partners. And I attended my first seminar in Paris. It was there that I realized that my life was going to change. Cooking in a kitchen for the rest of my life was over as of 1989. But this first experience shortly expired.

An associate suggested I complete a personality test. One thing led to another, and I began to delve into Scientology. This was something I had never heard of before, and I soon found myself in Copenhagen. The subject seemed interesting, discussing personal development and helping people to become free, rising through their programs. And, once again, I learned a lot.

This is where my character began to really assert itself because I drew from it what seemed most valuable to me, without entirely adhering to the Scientology philosophy. The negative aspects were that we worked endless hours with almost no freedom, very poor compensation, and total control. Yet, I persisted for over two years. I had become an essential element. I not only learned to use the computer tool, distributing all intranet messaging in the company, but I ended up managing their kitchen. And that is where I finally became autonomous in the kitchen and gained self-confidence!

I returned to France in 1993 and quickly found a job in direct sales for an internationally renowned German company. After four years, I performed well and became the agency's top salesman several times. I spearheaded an agency in Rennes, where I rose to sales coordinator in 1995, and one in Vannes. It was there that I met the woman who was to become my wife. We married in 1999, and my daughter was born soon after that.

With my acquired experience in sales, I belied the psychologist who had told just me a few years earlier that I was not made for sales. In 1997, I fulfilled a dream of mine—reconciling sales and cooking—by joining a regional company that sold frozen food products to professionals in the food trade! It was a great experience. I exploded the scores, increasing sales by 33% in May 1998.

But what was supposed to be a madly exciting step quickly turned into a nightmare. The new manager took advantage of a drop in sales to trick me into signing an amendment to the employment contract. I believed I would earn more commissions, but the opposite happened.

In the midst of all this, during an annual visit to the occupational physician, the doctor advised me to get vaccinated against hepatitis B on the pretext that I was in regular contact with food products. This was during a vaccination campaign. After the second injection, I woke to realize that I could no longer walk. I was diagnosed with multiple sclerosis.

At that time, I was fortunate to meet an "enlightened" doctor who made me read a few books and made several things aware to me. I do not know if it was the vaccine that caused it or the combination with the stress I was experiencing at the time. It still took a month to recover.

For me, it was unthinkable that this disease would take over. I had just started a career. I had found a path that I liked, and I was doing very well. I was winning markets! This company convinced me to return to Alsace to develop the region, but these were more promises that failed to materialize.

I chose food packaging. But my illness was manifesting itself more and more slyly, with loss of sensitivity, my balance becoming fragile, and my gait becoming more and more difficult.

Though not the best company, I remained loyal for seven years because I was beginning to lack the self-confidence to change and start again elsewhere. My deteriorating health only increased my worries. At one point, the stress of the poor atmosphere became too unbearable. So, I made a change one last time. This new company promised higher pay, but after fifteen months. But my body said "Stop!"

The end of my commercial career! I could no longer cope with the long commute and all the walking. I had a total of three crises in 2009.

But I refused to give up! I would not accept defeat! I still had my dream. I just knew something would come up.

I tried banking, but that was not it either. I felt in my soul that I deserved something else. And I believed that no employer deserved me. I had given too much and suffered too many betrayals and psychological bullying! I wanted to live and be free, to bring my light to the world. And I realized how much I'd learned during all these years through all the meetings and after years of research.

Despite my refusal to give up on my dream, the last crisis confined me to a wheelchair in 2014. Fatigue became increasingly challenging to manage. Financially, it was difficult. I ended up on a disability pension which dropped my income by half.

Luckily, my wife had her salary. But in 1995, she was found to have a brain tumor. An emergency operation followed with severe after-effects. She was never able to recover and fully return to work. She had also become disabled.

Fate continued to challenge us! The relentless setbacks felt extremely difficult. I wondered what the universe was trying to reveal to me. I recovered, but I must admit that doubt haunted me night and day. It was difficult to retain positive thoughts when so much had gone wrong.

I continued searching. After testing several products from various MLM companies, I found a technology that influences the cells. My extreme fatigue ended, after overwhelming me for several years with ever-increasing intensity, in no more than two weeks. Amazingly, more improvements followed. And, finally, a trustworthy company, with a high level of ethics and a genuine philosophy.

The last three years have shown continual improvement, economically and health-wise. My illness seems to have stopped progressing and I have resumed a full-time professional career from home.

For once in my life, I am enthusiastic about the future and extremely grateful for the progress I've made with associates and clients.

My journey has been painful and difficult: betrayals, setbacks, roadblocks, injustices, and unfairness at a level that made me want to just give up and quit on many, many nights. But taking on each obstacle, I discovered that I had choices: surrender, settle, make excuses, quit, or just give up.

But in those moments, I can tell you, I never gave up! I believed within the depth of my soul that whatever I had to face would somehow be worth it! And I determined that what did not kill me only made me stronger!

So, I'm not here to be exiled from your life by spouting hollow phrases and philosophy devoid of any meaning. In fact, that important mission I dreamed of was to be part of your life—right here, right now. You see, I have achieved the dream I made as that little boy so many years ago that *decided to believe in his great destiny*—that I would somehow get chosen to make a difference in your life. No, I could not have imagined the things I had to face to overcome the difficulties along the way. But I'm here, in this moment, to inspire you never to give up, to endure anything because the test is worth it, and that the challenges from life that do not kill you only make you stronger!

## BIOGRAPHY

Patrice Maurer knew from an early age that he would have an extraordinary destiny. Thanks to his solidly anchored belief, he has been able to persevere through every obstacle. It began with childhood bullies and continued through his professional career. The rollercoaster ended the moment he decided to change! The revelation that his life failed to correspond to what he had dreamed of achieving in life fuelled this decision. It took endless failures and soul-wrenching endurance to discover what he'd imagined in his mind. Today, after coming full circle back to his city of birth, Patrice lives his dream in the east of France with his amazing wife of over twenty years, Karine, and their wonderful daughter, Morgane.

Contact Patrice Maurer via https://linktr.ee/pakamosolutions

CHAPTER 27

# Higher Way Of Life

*By Patty Carson*

As I was driving from a long, life-altering business trip, I turned into a gas station to grab a snack, only to realize I was getting ready to drive over a big curve. At that moment, I jerked the steering wheel to turn back into my lane. It was so fast; the next thing I heard was a semi-truck honking its horn at me. I have no explanation except that it was a miracle that it didn't run right over the top of me! What I know is, at that moment, I was sure I wasn't sitting there for very long, but it felt as if a lifetime of memories and thoughts went flooding through my head.

My first thought was, "Oh my gosh! Just a few hours ago, I had a young girl riding with me who was going through a troubling time. She shared that she had seriously thought of taking her life twice but decided that next time she would just pull in front of a semi. I completely empathized with her because several years of hard knocks life threw at me made her story mine as well. Twice before, I had been rock bottom, and decided that next time, I would just pull in front of a semi and be done. At that moment, I felt, she was placed in my life for a reason, and I was called to something bigger than me!"

They say your life flashes before you in your last moments. I felt that is exactly what happened at that moment in time! In my early years, my parents and I lived in Oklahoma. Life had been fairly simple until the seventh grade. That was when I really learned that life isn't always fair. Until this time, my dad had been a tile setter. That was until his knee started swelling. One day, he couldn't even hold a cigarette in his hand. You pretty much needed your knees and hands to do his job. Now, his career was over, and we were financially broke. I vividly remember Mom and Dad picking me up from grandma and grandpa's farm in Kansas on a Friday. When we got home, they were fighting over money. My dad said he was going to hustle some pool with the last remaining $75. Mom was distraught and began crying. She grabbed a bottle of pills and went into her bedroom. I went to sleep, crying and thinking that she would be dead by the morning. Instead, she woke me up in the middle of the night to have my dad talk to me. He was obviously drunk and said, 'I've been out dancing, and I spent all of our money.' That was when my parents told me they were getting divorced, and they brought me to stay on my grandparents' farm in Kansas until they settled things out. Instead of getting divorced, Mom and Dad decided to stay together, and they moved to Kansas. This was my first lesson of "Tough times don't last, but tough people do!"

My parents taught me many life lessons. I know it wasn't easy for them to stay together. They were handed many hard knocks, but they neither gave up nor quit on each other! Obviously, they weren't perfect, but they instilled me with good lessons. We went to church every Sunday. They taught me the most important book one could read was the Bible. They also taught me to pray, to believe in God and miracles.

My parents got involved in network marketing when I was nine years old, so I was raised with this attitude of "If you can believe it, with hard work, you can achieve it!" They taught me the power of our dreams! We always had personal development books, and we listened to motivational tapes, which also helped mold my mind.

Growing up, grandpa was my hero. I remember telling him, 'When you die, I am going to die because I can't ever live without you!' I was twenty-four when I lost him, and this is where I learned a vital lesson about our thoughts and words and the power of life and death. Growing up Lutheran, we pick a Bible verse to follow us throughout our lives. Grandpa had lung cancer; he suffered in the hospital for exactly ten days, after which he died. After he died, I learned about the Bible verse he picked: "Fear none of those things which thou shalt suffer: behold, the devil shall cast *some* of you into prison, that ye may be tried; and ye shall have tribulation ten days: be thou faithful unto death, and I will give thee a crown of life" (Revelation 2:10). After learning his verse, I thought to myself, "Why would you pick a verse like that?" This was the time I reflected on my confirmation verse: "Ask and it will be given to you; seek and you will find; knock and the door will be opened to you" (Matthew 7:7). When I chose that verse, I remember thinking, 'If I have this verse, I will have everything I want in life!' Not quite true. There have been numerous trials and tribulations. But ultimately, I am blessed. After hearing grandpa's verse and how it came to fruition, I become obsessed with the power of our words.

I reflected on the time I met my husband Mark, and I told my mom when I was in the eighth grade, 'I'm going to marry him someday! He needs to grow up first, but I'm going to marry him someday!' <u>At the age of twenty, I got married to him.</u> While pregnant with my son, whenever anyone asked, 'Do you want a boy or a girl?' I would reply, 'I'm having a brown-eyed boy!' Guess what I got: a brown-eyed boy. I never made those proclamations with my two daughters, who have blue and hazel eyes.

What attracted me to my husband was that he was a dreamer! While dating, he built a dream that we would be retired millionaires by the time we were thirty. I believed him! However, four months after we got married, his father passed away, and I watched the light in his eye disappear, and his dreams slip away. The dream didn't stop for me. <u>Knowing it was going</u> to be a hard road, I was determined to make him believe again!

My first real understanding of networking was when I ran for County Treasurer. I ran a hard race; I was eight months pregnant with my oldest daughter, and I was tired. So, I decided I had done all I could the weekend before the primary. I lost by nine votes! I learned a very hard but crucial lesson. I gave up before the job was done. Had I gone all-out that weekend, I have no doubt I would have won. This was also the time that my grandpa was on his deathbed. The night before he died, he told me, "If you run a write-in campaign, you will win!" Two weeks before the election, I announced a write-in campaign. I networked with one hundred people to help me, and we won by over 200 votes. I say "we" because it was networking at its finest and teamwork made that happen!

I loved that job, but not the politics, so I started my business ventures. I was building a network marketing business with my husband. Our up-line lied to us, and my husband was done. Like most start-ups, I started a traditional business and was bankrupt within three years. After several failed attempts, I started raising dogs. I lost money there as well. I finally joined another company and made my way to the top. Finally, I felt like I had a big win, only to have the rug pulled out under me by a new CEO who was a retired two-star general and ran the company more like a military base than a volunteer army. My business eventually crumbled. My husband was so negative by this point; he didn't believe in me or my dreams anymore. I couldn't really blame him. My kids were all grown by this point, and I believed I had showed them nothing but failure. However, deep down, I didn't believe that because I remember my son writing "I am a Winner" on the top of every paper in grade school. The teachers would often reply with a smiley face or "Yes you are" on the top of his assignment!

Still very broken and unbelieving of my dreams coming true anymore, I got a call one day from my friend Andi, who told me, 'You need to pray about it, get up, dream again, and meet the founders of the company!' I did just that, and there I went again with another business venture. Why did I do this again, possibly setting myself up for more heartbreaks? I was stubborn and wanted to prove, once again, to my family that I could win. In order to not quit, I would say a prayer each morning before getting out of bed, 'Please, God. Bring in the people I am supposed to talk to, and I will do my job!' I believe the only way you really win in life is to have a servant's heart. You don't win alone; you win by helping others win! Before getting out of bed every morning, I would say, 'I'll be here a year from today!' I have a daily positive affirmation that I say: 'I have blessings coming from every direction, I don't know from where or why, but I will accept them and thank the Lord for them!'

One of the most valuable words of advice I was ever given is: "Don't compare yourself; run your own race!" It took me six years to hit the top position of my company! After learning that a goal without a deadline is just a wish, I proclaimed: 'By June 1, 2015, I will be at the top position of our company!' I made it! Next, I heard of an incentive trip to Costa Rica. I told my husband, 'We're going to Costa Rica!' He laughed. A few months later, we were in Costa Rica! The power of our words is more than we can imagine.

The following year, I said, 'We are going to be six-figure income earners in the company!' In July of 2016, one of my biggest dreams came true! We were going to be recognized as new $100K ring earners. We invited our kids to the event. My husband said all along that he was not going to talk. As our names were announced to come up on stage, my husband said, 'I'm talking first!' He took the mic and turned to the founders of the company, thanked them, and said he was glad I listened to them because we would have probably been one of those couples who wouldn't have made it. Then he looked at me and said, in front of 3,000 people, and most importantly, our three kids, 'I'm going to let the one who built this talk now: MY HERO!' These were the moments that flashed through my mind in those few seconds sitting in front of the semi. I had found my happy place and no longer had those thoughts. However, as I drove on, I thought, 'Man, Mark calling me his hero wasn't the end of my story!'

Since that time, I have had more hard balls thrown at me with my parents, a sudden tragic loss of my son-in-law leaving my youngest daughter widowed with two young children, and my 105-year-old grandma coming to live with me for nine months during her final journey in life. Life isn't always easy, but the lessons I learned from my 105-year-old grandma gave me the courage and confidence to become vulnerable, to share my story and her story, and to give hope. Stay tuned for the full book and, as Paul Harvey would say, 'The rest of the story!'

## BIOGRAPHY

Patty Carson is a professional business builder and network marketer with thirty-five years of experience. She won a write-in election when she was just twenty-four years old. She is a Nutritious Life Master Certified Coach. Patty has been featured in *Success From Home* magazine. She takes her experiences in life and business seriously and uses them to help people. Patty's passion is to inspire individuals to overcome the obstacles that hold them back and she teaches them to create a blueprint of their dreamlife. Patty has been a student of the hard-knocks university and has overcome problems using personal and leadership development for over forty years. Patty has professionally built herself to top leadership positions with two companies bringing millions in revenue to those companies and touching thousands of lives. Patty married her high school sweetheart Mark in 1984, and they share a son, two daughters, and four grandchildren.

Contact Patty Carson via https://linktr.ee/patty_carson

CHAPTER 28

# From Fear To Faithfulness

*By Philip Booth*

Rewinding back to the mid-1980s, I found myself standing on the main street of my hometown Te Puke in New Zealand. Although having only one main street, Te Puke has now become host to the main production of Kiwifruit in New Zealand and is exported worldwide. In 1933, Jim McLoughlin began to grow 'Chinese Gooseberries' and saw its potential as a marketable fruit by renaming it Kiwifruit. In that main street, as I stood outside a small home appliance store, which had been there since I completed my apprenticeship as a radio and TV serviceman in the mid-sixties in an adjacent store across the road, I said to myself, "I'd love to own this shop," little did I know what was in store for me. At that point, I was unaware that the voice inside me came from my own spirit as I didn't feature God in my life that much, let alone know we are spirit, soul, and body. I'd sometimes attend church during Easter and other occasions; however, God was not an important part of my life at that time. In retrospect, however, God was "on my case," and I unknowingly needed Him well before I acknowledged Him and his presence and had invited Him into my life.

Since I was about twenty-two, I had a desire to own a business. I desired to make a lot of money, even to become a millionaire. However, fear, a bad self-image, lack of self-worth and confidence, plus a low sense of achievement barred me from doing so. I even lacked the courage to do things my friends did, like surfing, as I was a poor swimmer.

Life was miserable right from when I started school. I recall one nasty teacher scolding me, striking me with her bony hands, saying she wasn't happy with my effort. I found learning difficult and considered myself a "dumb" boy. I did have some musical ability and learned to play the guitar. But I found it hard to practice as I had little real application and a desire to practice and relied on the fact that I had a natural gift in music to get by. When I was around ten years old, one of my teachers, who was a classical guitarist, noticed my natural ability and started giving me lessons along with another pupil. The boy's lack of talent amused me, and I'd think he'd never make it. While I went lax, the boy practiced even harder. Eventually, he became one of New Zealand's best guitarists. I made very little progress compared to him. Later in life, I reflected that one needs to hone their God-given talents and gifts with long hours of consistent practice. Even so, I did learn enough to join several bands in my youth as a rhythm guitarist, one of the bands was called "The Arms & Legs."

After I left high school in the sixties, I did an apprenticeship as a radio serviceman and progressed to television servicing, where my love for home appliances began to develop. I worked in the service division of a company that sold home appliances. In 1972, after completing my apprenticeship, I married my sweetheart of five years and worked in that same company for some years. However, I still desired to own my own business.

One day, I saw an advertisement for a television serviceman and an offer to buy into the business by a company located in a pulp and paper town near my hometown. The fact that I could buy into the business sparked my interest. I successfully interviewed for the job and shifted to the nearby town called Kawerau. I took my Mark 1 Ford Zephyr, my Triumph Saint motorbike, my Volkswagen car, and a piano with me. I joined the service company and began servicing the TV's around the area while my business partner serviced the refrigeration appliances. I was really attracted to the possibility of buying into the business. So that's what I did and then began working hard. Some years later, I talked my business partner into opening a retail home appliance store; I ran the retail department while he ran the service division. Despite my lack of retail experience, we did well but often had cash-flow problems and sometimes had to hold cheques back for payment, sometimes up to three months.

Being married, the babies started to arrive. Having three boys made my "hell-fear" even worse as I grappled with a father's responsibilities alongside my work. Then I failed, I did something very unwise, which troubled me greatly, and I fell into depression.

Life became even more hellish, and I felt my whole character was being challenged. I slept poorly as I had a hard time coming to terms with how I had failed. I was not handling things well and relied on tranquilizers every day. I joined a service club that did good work around town, trying to be someone. Personally, this didn't help my character much, but I made many friends.

Meanwhile, the Baptist church in town began to pray for the town's businesspeople, and the Pastor often purchased electronic bits and pieces from me. The Pastor and his congregation began praying for me. As they did, God began to draw me to him. For the first time, I began thinking of questions such as:

What is reality?
What is the meaning of life?
What is the purpose of my life?
Why am I here?

When I walked around the CDB in Kawerau, at times, I would come across Christian tracts lying on the ground. Reading them showed me how I could get in touch with God through his son Jesus Christ. I came across a Christian woman who had quite a testimony of her personal salvation. She shared scriptures with me. So, besides my bed one night, I prayed along the lines suggested in the tract and asked Jesus to come into my life and forgive all my sins. A weight fell off my shoulders, and the light seemed to increase in the room. I stepped out into the night, looked up into the sky, and it was as if the heavens were revealing the presence of God. What an experience!

God's love flooded my soul.

I realized my purpose, my calling, and my self-worth.

A new chapter had begun in my life, and I felt like I wanted to return to my hometown. My business partner at the time accepted that I wanted to leave the business and bought out my shares in the company that we had started together.

I returned to Te Puke in 1983 and joined a church, being highly active in the music department and preaching also and where I remain to this day. The original Pastors, now deceased, were responsible for much of my training as a Christian.

Once back in Te Puke, I reached out to God, asking if it was His will that I go back into business again. As I prayed, I realized I was trying to make a deal with Him. So, I left the decision in His hands and hoped that He'd give me a sign. The next day, I went to a store downtown, where I found a Christian book stand. My eyes caught a book (whose name I forget) written by Televangelist Dr. Robert Schuller, the creator of Hour of Power. As I began to read the phrases of positivity, I felt God's affirmation.

Then, I headed to the company where I had done my apprenticeship for a scheduled interview as I had been offered a job there earlier that week. I took the owner's absence as God's will and left, thinking that the job was not for me. So, I headed to the shop whose owner wanted to sell out. This was the same shop I had stood in front of and had felt a tug in my heart to own, and right now, I felt the current owner's willingness to do so was God's will for me to buy the business. So, I decided on it, but not without some fear. It was as though I became double-minded for a while a few days later. I discussed it with my brother, and he commented about my "getting cold feet." I recognized it for what it was and went on to complete the purchase. Buying the business cost $18,000, as it had been run down by the previous owner who had problems with it. I prayed that I'd be able to pay the bills on the 20th of every month. I'm now happy to say that was never an issue.

I was quite apprehensive on my first day, but I got through, thanking God quietly in my office at the end of the day. The peace from this assured me that owning this business was God's approval to go back into business.

During this time, I was still with my first wife, with whom I had three children. Eventually, because of the damage I had caused to our relationship, she left me, leaving me with our sons for a time; however, being a good mother, she would spend time with them on the weekends. This was in early 1984, and by 1986, despite asking God to reunite us, I was divorced. God never goes against the will of anyone, and so my marriage was not restored. Committed to Jesus, I then focused on letting him speak through the Bible to me. Over the next ten years, God allowed me to dig out many negative aspects of my life. I'm happy to report I'm not anything like my old negative self. Thank God for that!

Over time, my shop became way too small due to God's blessings, as I had learned the scriptural principles of finance. I found a bigger building three shops away. It housed a much bigger shop area, two other smaller shops on the bottom floor, and three shops upstairs. This was a huge opportunity for me, with real potential to grow. Under God's direction and via some help from a financier, I made an offer for the building. It was accepted. However, the seller wanted me to add the GST (10% of the price negotiated at the time). My financier agreed on the exceptional deal, and I got the bigger building complete with existing tenants. The GST content came back to me, which I spent on refurbishing the area. People were amazed at our opening. They sent flowers and letters, and some appreciated that I restored a rundown building, today worth over one million dollars. My original loan is long paid-off. I have a mortgage-free home and a rental property short of a few payments before it's mine.

My business experienced growth, along with some trials, especially during the financial crash of 2008. Despite a devalued bottom line, I did not lay anyone off. God remained faithful and heard my prayers. At times where I'd be short ($30,000) on the month's bills, my good friend and employee Tom and I prayed together; and the money was always there. Tom and I enjoyed many years together (1984-2015), praying at the start of the business day and thanking God at the end of the day for prosperity in our business, region, our families, and the families of all those who worked there. In November of 2010, the news that Kiwifruit canker (Psa) had been found in an orchard in Te Puke went viral as it threatened the viability of Kiwifruit in New Zealand as it could have completely wiped out every existing vine and destroyed the multimillion-dollar industry as it had already done in other nations. Being a severe threat to our area and retail sector and, of course, my own business, I inquired of the Lord. His reply was to say, "I am going to bless the Kiwifruit Industry." To make a long story short, he did, and the Kiwifruit Industry continues to thrive, which is another proof of God's love and faithfulness for people.

In 2013, my desire for marriage was stronger than ever, so I went to Nanning, China, to meet a Chinese lady. I stayed there for a couple of weeks, getting to know her, which was difficult as she knew very little English, and I, very little Mandarin. Nevertheless, we still liked each other. I returned to New Zealand to get her into the country. But it never worked out. I read this as an indication from God that He had other plans for me.

In 2014, I fell into depression after having surgery done on my prostate for cancer. This bout of depression taught me why people are driven to suicide. For myself, I couldn't understand why, even as a Christian and God in my life, I was so depressed. I thought it would never pass as everything seemed dark, but I didn't come close to suicide. To make things worse, I had an employee who tried to take me over, telling me he prayed to God for this to happen. His manipulative attitude made my life difficult. I'm happy to say nothing transpired. However, over the years, I've had many awesome people work for me, and we've all had great relationships that exist to this day.

Returning to my birthplace made me realize that God has a plan for our lives and even a geographical place in mind. Relationships with the right people are crucial to that plan's working. With God's help, I've been able to serve my community through my work. Even before the COVID-19 pandemic, more so during and after, people wanted to "shop local" and were eager to see that I did not shut down. I remember reading years ago that the benchmark for greatness in business is gauged in the level of service given to their customers.

I've been in business since 1983 when it went through various names: Phil Booth TV & Audio; Phil Booth Appliance Court; Phil Booth Retravision; and Phil Booth Appliance Spot. My current retail business is called "100% Phil Booth." Being seventy now, I feel like I'm only getting started and have no intention of retiring. I still enjoy my business immensely.

After waiting on God from 1986, after my divorce, to 2018 for a wife of His choosing, He brought along a beautiful Vietnamese woman with two children aged thirteen and ten. We are so happy and compatible that my heart swells with joy. She was well worth waiting for. My parents have passed away, but hers are still alive and only a few years younger than me. I have gained two stepsons, some parents-in-law, two more brothers-in-law, and their families, all based in Hanoi.

Additionally, I have eight grandchildren from my own family. My new wife and I were married on 6 October 2018, and a year later, she found she had nasopharyngeal cancer. But that's another story!

From fear to faithfulness: the faithfulness I refer to is God's faithfulness to those who have committed their lives to Him despite feelings of helplessness and failure. God vivifies that which otherwise might have been destroyed, and He delights being part of people's lives—His creation. He says, "Delight yourself in the Lord . . . and He will give the desires of your heart."

The Bible says, "A faithful man who can find?" Yet, in God, faithfulness is possible. All is accomplished by faith. Fear is the total absence of faith. Every day in God is a fresh start.

"Commit your way to the Lord, and He will cause your thoughts to come in line with His will, and so shall your plans be established and succeed." God always leads us to victory. Because of this fact, 1983 was indeed a brand new start in life for me, and the fears that dogged me in my early life have left for good, all due to God's faithfulness. Even the fear of lack has left me as God proved his faithfulness in that area by ensuring that I always had sufficient to pay my bills, and that was an answer to prayer. My DREAM to own my own business came into reality by daring to believe God and trusting in his faithfulness.

## BIOGRAPHY

Philip Booth is the proprietor and CEO of 100% Phil Booth. He has been a retailer of home appliances for forty years. His career began after completing his Trade Certificate as a radio and television serviceperson, after which he launched a career in retailing. He has owned and managed two businesses, and his longevity has resulted from leveraging the two top appliance co-operating companies in New Zealand and a strong faith in the goodness of God. He currently belongs to the Appliance Connexion Group Services Ltd, which is associated with the NARTA Group of Australasia. Phil has kept up with current appliance retailing trends by traveling extensively to conferences hosted by various groups and suppliers of appliance brands, CEOs, visits to appliance factories, and listening to motivational guest speakers.

Contact Philip Booth via https://linktr.ee/philbooth

CHAPTER 29

# Growing A Side Business Into A Full-Time Income

*By Phillipa Nanyondo Wavamunno Byamah*

I stood behind the stage as the MC bellowed out my short bio over the microphone while the crowd of thousands eagerly awaited what I had to say. At that moment, I wondered if it really could be me they were waiting for. If it *was* me in the wings, waiting to step onto this big international stage with members from different countries, how on earth had I arrived at that point? Was it really me, ready to teach, inspire, and share my story? You see, no one would have believed a few years ago that I would have got so far, as my journey had always seemed to be one of going against the odds. It started with faith as small as a mustard seed—and a little determination.

As a child, I always wanted to do something with my life and feared not having the choices I needed to succeed. I had seen both worlds of having and not having a lot. And I trusted the God I serve who says we are made to thrive not to survive.

Growing up in a family of eight children, four boys and four girls, my father taught us that working hard for what we wanted to achieve was the key to success. He endeavored to educate us at the best schools in the country and sacrificed everything in his power to ensure we had the best in life. During my secondary and high school education, it soon became apparent I possessed a natural gift for scientific subjects and had a keen liking for and ability to solve mathematical problems. Later on, taking on a BSc in Quantitative Economics on a government sponsorship also proved easy for me. Indeed, that young girl slowly grew out of her playfulness and began taking her academic performance very seriously. It surprised my parents that I was regularly at the top of my class, especially in math exams.

I started my first job in the banking industry, even before fully graduating. My keen eye for detail and enthusiasm for learning about what went on in the different departments saw me being regularly promoted, ending up in the Credit department. I also moved banks in pursuit of a more satisfying professional career. As I pursued more goals in life, I started to tell myself that doing even more was possible. As a wise person said, "The 1st step towards getting somewhere is to decide that you are not going to stay where you are."

I started my first 'side hustle' shortly after I joined the corporate world. I had quickly embarked on saving a good percentage of my small salary, and I pondered where to invest it most profitably. After accumulating some funds, I launched a special car hire business: I bought a second-hand vehicle that wasn't in good mechanical condition.

***My first lesson****: If you think of an idea, don't wait for a 'perfect time' to put it into action. Just take the first step and get started. There's never a perfect time or perfect conditions. Just start with whatever you have and take a leap of faith. Also, learn to start small, as from small and humble beginnings come greater things. In my case, by starting early in coming up with different ideas for creating avenues of earning an additional income, I used the vital lesson of taking the first step of faith and starting anyway. I didn't wait for perfect conditions, and neither did I wait to have a lot of money; I just got started with what I had. And that started my journey of learning from my business mistakes.*

*"Courage isn't about knowing the path,*
*it's about taking the first step "*—Katie Davis

I hired out the vehicle I'd bought for someone to drive it as a taxi, and they were supposed to pay me a certain amount of money weekly, although I would cover the mechanical and servicing costs. This worked well for the first few weeks until the 'stories' from the driver as to why he couldn't pay me started and seemed endless. From one mechanical failure to another, I soon found that I was shelling out more in repair and servicing costs than I had revenue coming in. Reluctantly, I decided I had to give up that particular dream and let the car go.

Next, I started a motorbike business, where I bought a new bike and hired it out in almost the same arrangement as with the previous car business. In my country, Uganda, motorcycle transport can be lucrative, as bikes ease transportation in congested city centers. But I soon began to get the same 'stories' from the motorcycle driver as I had from the taxi driver, and the epitome was when police confiscated the motorbike over some breach of traffic rules. The procedure to resolve the issue was not only lengthy but also costly and, once again, I soon had to give it up.

*My lesson number two*: *Before embarking on any business, consult experts in that area. I ventured into the transport business, which I knew for sure could be lucrative, without first getting any advice from a successful special hire (taxi) operator. Neither did I consult anyone who was successful in the motorcycle business. I relied on hearsay, and soon I was learning on the job—the hard way. The people I picked to partner with me took advantage of my partial ignorance, which meant my initial, unsuccessful forays into business became the first lessons learned on my side business journey.*

Identifying my next business venture was not difficult: I have always been a busy person who won't settle for less than I think is right. I always endeavored to complete my daily workload, tasks, and even projects before their deadlines, and I would soon be asking, 'what's next?'

*The habit of keeping aside part of my salary as savings for future investments enabled this journey of growing my part-time businesses into full-time income sources.* **And this makes my lesson number three:** *there are many times when we have big ideas and want to jump in to realize them (without experience) in a similarly big way. Lack of starting capital should* never be an excuse not to start a business; if you believe in what you're doing, then make it happen by putting aside some savings to enable your dream to come true.

We need to realize that whereas it's good to save, you have to learn to let your money grow and, in turn, allowing it to work for you. Before you identify and embark on a business that you will invest in for a better return, it is advisable not to have your savings sited long on a savings accounts but rather invest it in other avenues that will give you a better return like fixed deposits, government instruments like Treasury bills and bonds, umbrella trust funds and other Insurance packages among others. That way, your money earns more for you, interest is compounded, and you start earning more in interest on your original deposit. Never underestimate the value of money and time, taking on Life Assurance plans or education plans (if you have children) will save you so much in the future. This is a hustle-free way of getting your net worth to increase, one shilling after another. Recognize the compounding power of money—*that was my lesson number four.*

I have an eye for turning passions, talent, pain, and gaps in the market into opportunities. My next business venture was one I started because of my husband's love for popcorn. He loved fresh popcorn so much that I wanted to ensure he could always enjoy this treat whenever he wanted to. But our nearest supermarket didn't have a fresh popcorn machine, and I saw an opportunity to regularly supply my husband with fresh popcorn and make some extra income from the business idea of having a fresh popcorn machine at our local supermarket. I learned two lessons from this venture:

**Lesson five:** *Opportunities to make money are around you. You just have to look with 'smart eyes' and you will see them.*

**Lesson six:** *Never undermine a job that will earn you an extra income. Often, we suffer from the 'I am too cool' syndrome—wrongly thinking that some jobs are not meant for a certain class of people.*

Although I was already working in the banking sector and climbing the corporate ladder, I had no shame about taking on a fresh popcorn business. After a short time of supplying fresh popcorn to this one supermarket, doors soon opened to all its other outlets, and I found myself supplying other items to their outlets all across the country and in their Kenyan outlets as well. So, I approached two other supermarkets and expanded my supply chain. The money I earned through this venture meant we could easily pay our monthly expenses without touching our regular salaries.

In 2016, after a long December break spent in the traditional activities of visiting grannies and family, which we loved doing, we set out to do something different by deciding to have a family vacation. I had always loved travel, and I felt we needed to start living life with our kids and creating some different kinds of memories. After doing lots of research, this dream landed me in my next adventure, which would allow me to travel the world and gain an extra-income stream derived from multi-level marketing techniques. Of course, I didn't hesitate, given that working on any project I was passionate about was bound to be enjoyable. I learned that business models were changing, and companies were using MLM or word of mouth to get the word out about their products and services.

I decided to embark on this business and learn everything I needed by finding appropriate coaches and mentors to follow. It's important to follow people who have what you want and then do exactly what they do to become like them. I decided to get into student mode and learn as much as I could from my virtual mentors. I was coachable and trainable and applied everything I learned. I also found an accountability partner, with whom I shared my goals and visions, and I was held accountable for the daily activities and tasks I was supposed to fulfill.

Have you ever wondered how some people have this ability to handle many tasks at the same time and do all of them quite well?

Well, I tried to master the art and science of personal effectiveness. With the determination I had to succeed, I knew I first had to understand how to segment daily tasks and activities and prioritize important things directly related to achieving my visions and goals. I started slowly cutting back on certain activities that I realized had been taking up a lot of my time but were not actively contributing to my bigger goals. I became more intentional with life, as I tried to squeeze as much out of each day as possible to be more productive and effective. By doing a lot in the short time allotted to me for the day, I also learned how to delegate and empower people. I began to utilize the strong support system surrounding me. From home to my formal workplace and my side businesses, what became evident to me was that working alone, I could travel fast, but by standing on the shoulders of giants, I could go much further and also see farther. Based on this, I started to help people in my organization, and the more I helped others, the more I became better and saw better results for myself.

So, that day as I stood behind the stage as the host and Master of Ceremonies for the day bellowed my name, inviting me to come up on the stage and share my life experiences about how I got to the top of my organization and succeeded in turning my side business into a full-time income that helped me build my retirement portfolio, I pondered once more the past years of struggle and hard work, the sleepless nights of planning, the long meetings, the endless phone calls, meeting clients, attending training sessions, then driving through traffic jams to get home late, often way past the bedtimes of my beautiful children. I knew for sure I had sacrificed a lot to get to where I was. And I knew that there is always a trade-off in life and that, for me to break through and succeed in ensuring my family's future security and comfort, nothing was more important than making those positive life changes.

## BIOGRAPHY

Phillipa Nanyondo Wavamunno Byamah is an economist, banker, public speaker, performance specialist, entrepreneur, and business coach. She is an independent-minded, self-motivated, and versatile professional who seeks and achieves purpose-filled results in sometimes uncertain circumstances. Phillipa's enormous potential to thrive, to lead others, and her willingness to help others achieve their highest potential has been her calling in life. While rising in both her banking and business careers, she has traveled extensively to speak and motivate others, always striving to give of her best in their service, and has been rewarded with numerous related accolades, including achieving the top rank of her network marketing company. Her visionary leadership has mentored many around her, allowing them to experience great business and life success. She endeavors to leave a little piece of herself everywhere she goes. She lives in Uganda with her husband and two adorable children, Nahereza (God gives) and Kansiimeruhanga (I give thanks to God).

Contact Phillipa Nanyondo Wavamunno Byamah via https://linktr.ee/phillipawavah

CHAPTER 30

# Finish What You Start

*By Regina Nunnally*

In 1987, I was in Tae Kwon Do for quite a while, about four years or so. I wanted to quit, but I was genuinely scared to tell my father. I dreaded the tongue-lashing I would receive. But I didn't care; my heart wasn't in it. I was simply going through the motions. This situation went on for a few weeks, before I finally mustered enough courage to tell my daddy the truth. All that day at school, it was on my mind; my heartbeat speeded up, and my head started hurting when I thought about it. This was the day I was going to tell my father I wanted to quit going to Little Dragons Tae Kwon Do Center. What explanation would I give? How could I make things sound so bad that he would go along with it?

I got home, and he came out to take me to class. I told him flat out, "Daddy, I want to quit." There it was; I'd said it. The sky didn't come crashing down and, to my surprise, my daddy didn't say a word. It was opposite to what I'd expected. He wasn't all hail, fire, and brimstone. He simply said, "Okay." What? My daddy was not tripping over me for quitting?

I felt relieved, but then he said, "But you have to give back all the trophies, certificates, belts, and medals you've earned." Huh? Did he just say give back the trophies I'd won in tournaments, the Certificates of Achievement I'd received for training with some of the best martial arts teachers around, the belts I'd earned sparring with my instructor, who was a professional kick-boxer? I immediately recalled all the black eyes, chipped teeth, sprained fingers and toes, the jammed jawbone, and the shin knots I'd received in training. It was as though I again felt all those painful moments and emotions attached to these precious memorials.

I asked him why. He answered, "Because you won't want anything to remind you of the fact that you quit." Boom! There it was. I heard the disappointment in his voice, but I also heard regret. You see, my father dropped out of school when he was in the tenth grade. Over the years, he attempted to launch numerous businesses, all of which failed. There were probably more things he wished he'd done but hadn't—because when it got hard, he quit. So, in a way, he was living through me. He saw potential in me that I didn't see. Then he said, "You're too close to black belt. Get your black belt and then do what you want. Do it for me." So, in December 1988, I received my black belt. It was a big deal—I did it for my daddy. Then, in May 1989, the day after Mother's Day, my daddy died.

## Challenge #1

I was sixteen and a junior at Mainland Senior High School when my dad left my mama and me behind. We had his homegoing service the following Saturday morning. I went to my junior prom that same evening. I didn't feel like going but was encouraged to go by my peers. Plus, I could hear my daddy saying, "One monkey doesn't stop the show." He never got to see me dressed up, looking pretty. That was one of the hardest days of my life. I buried my father that morning and attended the junior prom that same evening.

## Challenge #2

During my senior year, I accepted some terrible advice from my school counselor. I was on track to graduate Cum Laude. My grades during the first semester of my senior year would be the determining factor in maintaining that track. I was eligible to apply for a scholarship, but I needed classes to be competitive. So, I rearranged my schedule. I took physics, honors chemistry, and trigonometry to qualify. I totally bombed it. I was so close and had worked so hard for almost four years, and then one semester took me out of the game. My grade point average dropped. When my friends got their caps and gowns and honor cords, I did not get mine. One of them even asked me where mine were. "Denied," I said; I'd missed the mark. But my father's words still rang in my ears—"Finish what you start!" The second semester was better, but it was too late. I graduated with honors, but I had missed the mark for graduating Cum Laude. That experience left a bitter aftertaste in my mouth. I felt robbed and cheated. I felt defeated, but I decided in my heart to finish what I started as best as I could.

**Challenge #3**

I decided to go to law school. To apply, you must take the law school admissions test or LSAT. However, out of ignorance, I didn't take it seriously enough. I underestimated the difficulty entirely. My 'friend' was pursuing the same course as me, but we never really shared much. So, I guess it was all on me. I studied the day before, walked in, took the test, and did miserably—ending up with a low score. However, I thought I still had a shot at getting into my alma mater, the University of Florida, so I applied. My friend applied and was accepted. I was denied admission. I applied to four other schools, who also rejected my applications.

I took the LSAT twice after that. In the middle of the second test, my brain started to freeze up. I'd read a paragraph, then start losing my concentration. The words on the paper wouldn't make sense to me, which had never happened before. In the end, I'd walked out of the test early, lying to the proctor by telling her I was sick. I cried on the way home.

Then, one day, a revelation came to me: I figured that I would stay motivated by surrounding myself with reminders of what I wanted to achieve. So, I contacted several law offices and volunteered my services. The local legal aid office accepted my invitation, and I volunteered to interview potential clients. Then, the director suggested I talk to a local judge. I arranged that, and the judge became my mentor. Being around the very thing I was pursuing, studying law, kept me focused. During the third testing, I met a guy who gave me an application form for a new law school opening in Orlando. I applied and, in May 1997, I received my admissions letter to attend The University of Orlando School of Law.

**Challenge #4**

Studying for the bar meant working anywhere between six to eight hours a day, although the rules have changed significantly now. Back then, there were eight subjects to review. The test was in two parts of six hours each. That meant twelve hours in total, with two days reading and answering two-hundred questions and writing essays. The bar test is so extreme that they even have EMS standing by on the scene. I became a bar rep, running study sessions, so I could afford to take the exam. I watched the training videos during the day, then my roommate and I would watch them again at night. Before taking the real bar exam, I took two practice exams. I needed a 131 to pass; I made a 128 on the real exam. I failed! Couldn't they have found three more points? It was so frustrating.

So, I asked God for a plan to succeed, and this is what He showed me: I should start with my weakest subject first, which was Evidence. I read the section and did all the practice questions. Then, I went on to my next weakest subject, property, reading the material, and adding more practice questions. I was soon walking around with a stack of index cards filled with questions and answers that I took everywhere I went. I even studied them in church, in the choir, during a sermon. Before I studied, I prayed Joshua 1:9, which says, "Be strong, be of good courage . . . the Lord God is with you wherever you go."

On the day of the exam, which lasted three hours, I flew through the first part comprising one-hundred questions. My studying meant I could see patterns in the questions that made the answers flow like a stream. I finished early and walked out jubilant. I was blown away.

After lunch, I sat down, ready to knock out the second half of the exam. I prayed my scripture, got working, but then hit a brick wall. About every third or fourth question, I got stuck. I started to feel a little anxious. I struggled through the second half and didn't finish early that time. For two long months, I waited on the results. When the day finally came, my heart was pounding because it was do or die for me. The results were being posted on the bar website, so I signed in. And there it was—I'd passed. When I received my letter in the mail, my score was 147, more than enough to pass the exam.

**Life Lessons**

First, never underestimate your plans to meet your goals. You need to take it seriously. I realized in my early years that I was not preparing myself properly to meet my goals. Partly due to ignorance and arrogance. I heard someone say that blame is a way to discharge pain and discomfort. I can't blame anyone else for my shortcomings and take ownership of them. If you enjoy eating humble pie, I strongly recommend sticking to the plan. Success is in your hands!

Second, learn how to encourage yourself. No matter how hard, no matter how ugly it seems, remember the words of those who have your best interests at heart. I challenge you to speak the words over your life—you must allow the inspiration of others to penetrate your heart. But be careful not to take pain as your guide; if you do, the antidote to your situation won't work. Your heart will become hard and nothing good will be able to take root there. Remember, a closed mind does not get fed.

Third, take action. People spoke into my life. I took action. I received revelations from God in the middle of my dry moments. I took action. The word of encouragement came; I took action. I got advice and direction; I took action. All those years ago, when my father advised me not to quit practicing Tae Kwon Do, I took action. Remember, A-C-T-I-O-N stands for A Challenge That Includes Opportunities Now!

Fourth, learn to thrive where you're planted. Studying for the bar was tough enough, but I determined in my heart not to let it devour my soul. Failing the bar was embarrassing; however, I kept my head high and pressed on. Every time you face a challenge, don't forget to live.

Embrace the moment until your change comes. Remember, it's only a temporary setback setting you up for a permanent comeback.

In conclusion, as a lawyer for over seventeen years now, I take action for my clients with a passion that gives them confidence. I wanted the pain and disappointment to stop. Those torment times directed me to meet great people who continue to mentor me in business and encourage me to cultivate myself to become a judge. You have to keep moving, my friend. You've come too far to turn around, and you're too close to your goal to quit now.

Keep the faith and stay the course. I am rooting for you. Purpose in your heart to finish what you start!

## BIOGRAPHY

Regina Nunnally is an author, criminal defense attorney, pastor, community leader, character actress, motivational speaker, and travelista entrepreneur. Born and raised in the Funshine State, Daytona Beach, Florida, Regina is a contributing author to the Amazon publishing bestseller *Daily Dose of Direction for Women in Business*. She has contributed articles to *Program Success* magazine and *Nia* magazine and collaborated on a story for an audio series called Confinement Chronicles Volume III, presented by Angie BEE Productions. Regina has been a featured speaker at the Healing the Whole Woman Conference and is scheduled to be a featured speaker/travel expert at an upcoming engagement called Map Out Your Life 2.0 in October 2020.

Regina Nunnally's contact details are available at https://linktr.ee/seetheworldthrumyeyes

CHAPTER 31

# Help Wanted: Hire Yourself

*By Reginald Dockery*

Many people dream of freedom, financial freedom, job freedom, and even time freedom. Before you dream it, I want you to contemplate the question: What is freedom? With most jobs, you're told what time to come in, what time to leave, what time to take a break, and what time to take lunch. Your employer also approves, or not, the time you can go on vacation or take personal days. Does that sound like freedom to you? There are several ways to be free, both financially and in your career path. These days, to have financial and time freedom, you will need multiple streams of income. The average millionaire has a minimum of seven streams or avenues of income.

In this chapter, I will examine many of those avenues: You can hire yourself as an employee, which is being self-employed. Then there's hiring yourself as a CEO or president, in which case, you are an owner and overseer. I'll show you how to answer the "Help Wanted" sign within you. I've heard several multimillionaires say, "You can never become wealthy or financially independent working a regular 9 to 5 job for someone else." So, I tell you to search within yourself today and answer your own "Help Wanted" sign.

We all have things we love to do. Maybe you love to write? Maybe taking photos makes you feel like a million dollars? Or perhaps you love crafting hand-made signs? I'm talking about the thing that makes you feel alive, your passion, what creates a fire in your bones.

But it's hard to believe you can ever make money from your passion. Surely, you think, I can't make money doing [insert your passion]. Nobody would pay me to do that. It's too much fun, and I love it too much. No way could I make money doing that.

That's where you're wrong. Today, thanks to the internet, almost any passion can be turned into a profitable side hustle.

Did you catch that?

You can make money doing the things you love most. Yep, you can turn your passion project into a profitable project. We all could use some extra cash in our lives. We've got bills to pay, kids to send to school, car repairs to make, and a dozen other expenses. Some extra cash could be useful and go a long way toward making our lives easier. This is where hiring yourself is crucial.

If you're interested in 'get rich quick' schemes, then this book is not for you. Because here's the reality: Creating a profitable business takes time, diligence, hard work, blood, sweat, and tears (well, hopefully, not too many tears!)

If you want to succeed with your life as a CEO, prepare to put in some work. You shouldn't expect to start operating and immediately have boatloads of cash pouring in. You need to be ready to put in many hours of work over the long-haul.

How do you generate the motivation needed to put in all that hard work? Look at your life as it currently is. Are you living your best life now? Are you completely fulfilled with your day job? Are there other things you would love to do to make money? Do you see others doing what you want to do?

If you're not living your best life now, let that serve as a motivator for your own business. You really can make money doing what you LOVE. You can generate significant income doing something that brings great satisfaction into your life.

How would it change your life if you were doing work that made you happy? How would it revolutionize things for you if you enjoyed the work you do every day?

To increase motivation for your business, envision what a successful outcome would look like for your side hustle. Paint a picture in your mind of what your best life will look like.

First, you need to get very clear on the answers to these questions:
- How badly do you want to succeed in your own company?
- What benefits do you want to experience?
- How will the extra cash you earn help you?
- What joy will you experience from doing what you love?

If you're not highly motivated to make your business a reality, it won't happen. Because here's the truth: Your Business will take you away from other good things that you could be doing.

You may need to give up some of the following:
- Watching television
- Your favorite reality shows
- Hobbies
- Spending too much time on the internet
- Time spent with friends

You may even need to sacrifice time usually spent with your family, although I don't recommend doing that over the long haul.

The point is simply that you will have to make sacrifices to make your business a reality. You're going to have to do the hard work necessary. You must be willing to give up some of the good things to achieve a great thing.

Most people don't realize that it usually takes a significant amount of time and work before you start making good money from your side hustle.

Success happens over the long haul, not overnight. If you want your business to be profitable, you must be willing to make sacrifices until you finally reach your objective.

World-famous soccer player Pele said: "Success is no accident. It is hard work, perseverance, learning, studying, sacrifice, and most of all, love of what you are doing, or learning to do." If you want to succeed, you must be willing to work hard and persevere. The good news is that if you persevere, you will almost certainly succeed.

All that being said, you must be confident that you can do it. If you constantly doubt yourself, you'll have a hard time getting traction. But if you have faith in yourself and believe firmly in your abilities, you truly can achieve great things.

The best time to start a business is right now. Don't wait any longer. There will never be a perfect time to get started. Start working on your project today, and adjust as time goes on. So, how do you identify what your business should be? How do you know what you should invest your time in? How can you determine the best activities to focus on? It's simple: You start by identifying the things you're most passionate about and interested in.

A business is the intersection of passion and profit. In other words, it's all about taking the things you love and are good at and turning them into a profitable gig. So, the first step is to identify what you love to do AND are good at doing. Both elements are required. If you want your business to be sustainable, you must love doing it. If you don't, you'll burn out quickly. When hard work and sacrifices are needed, you won't want to make them. A successful business involves an activity that you love doing.

You must also be good at your passion. In other words, you must have the necessary skill set to make it a reality. If you're not good at creating your product or performing your service, others simply won't want to pay you for it.

Ask yourself these questions:

- What do you love doing?

- What have people told you that you're good at?
- What do you lose track of time doing?
- What valuable skills do you have that people would pay for?
- What needs can you meet?

These questions will help you find the intersection of passion and profit. They will help you determine both your skillset and what you love. When these two things combine, you have a viable side hustle.

There is a psychological concept called "Flow." This is when you find yourself so immersed in an activity that you lose all track of time and are simply focused on what's in front of you. Your mind isn't distracted at all. Rather, you simply "flow" with your activity.

When do you find yourself in the "flow" of things? Pay attention to these moments. It's these activities that could be turned into sustainable companies.

Unless you're building something completely new and revolutionary, you're going to be competing against others. Whether you're selling a widget or offering coaching services, there will always be others against whom you're competing for business.

If you're going to succeed with your occupational passion, you must first find a way to differentiate yourself from your competitors. In other words, figure out how you're going to stand out from the crowd, how you're going to attract customers, how your offer is different and better than your competitor's.

How can you differentiate yourself from your competitors? There are numerous ways, including:

- Enhanced quality products or services
- Superior customer service
- Speedier delivery
- Less expensive products or services

- Higher or lower profit margins
- A noble cause you support with profits from your product

For example, let's say you're selling skin moisturizer online. You could create a unique skin moisturizer of better quality than most other skin moisturizers. Because your skin moisturizer is of better quality, you can sell it for a higher price and make higher profit margins.

Or you could sell your skin moisturizer at a discount and sell a higher volume. Or you could create an aggressive online marketing campaign designed to get your skin moisturizer ad seen by more people than your competitors.

If you don't find a way to differentiate yourself from your competitors, there's no reason why customers should purchase from you rather than them. You absolutely must find a way to stand out in the crowd.

All successful people are optimistic, and all optimistic people are usually, in one way or another, sooner or later, successful in accomplishing their life goals. Optimistic people tend to say "the glass is half-full," not "half-empty." They believe the whole universe is friendly towards them and is helping them in achieving their dreams. However, what many people tend to do is remain optimistic until they're just about to reach their goal. Then, they lose patience, become victims of criticism, and turn their back on the goal, resisting when it tries to pull them back in. This is why there isn't a success story for every dreamer or a rags-to-riches story for every poor person.

When Bill Gates was asked, if he found a dollar bill on the ground, would he bother picking it up? He said he would. Warren Buffett responded to the same question by saying that if Bill Gates missed picking up the dollar bill, he himself wouldn't. It's not as though they are hungry for money, but rather the optimistic mindset through which they perceive events that have led them to be among the world's wealthiest people today.

Wisdom of the early twentieth century:

The successful people of the early twentieth century had so much optimism that many of today's entrepreneurs regard them as their teachers, even if they haven't met them in person. For instance, W. Clement Stone has been described as a paranoid, not the type you find in an asylum, but what's called an inverse paranoid. While a classic paranoid believes the world is plotting to do him harm, Stone believed the world was plotting to do him good. He looked for opportunities in every challenging or difficult situation and used those opportunities to empower and enrich himself or advance his causes. In one of his famous books, Napoleon Hill mentioned these golden words: "Every adversity, every failure, and every heartache carries with it the seed of an equal or greater benefit."

Henry Ford was a highly optimistic entrepreneur, who believed if we think we can do a thing, or we think we can't do a thing, either way, we're all right. So, it's not the type of problem or obstacle in our way that matters but our attitude towards it that matters and determines whether we can proceed towards our goals.

But why are we all right either way, according to Ford?

In other words, the question is, does positive thinking work, or is it just a pseudo-scientific idea? If you think and believe you can't do something or can't accomplish a task within a particular time, you simply won't. However, if you think you can or constantly tell yourself you can and come to believe it, when your mind says, "Yes, you can!" then you're more likely to do the things necessary to make it happen. First, you must establish an objective or goal for your life. Success is purpose-driven. Hence, to be a successful person, you need to have precise intentions. Since we have different desires and passions, you need to figure out what yours is and discern what makes you happy, then use them as a source of motivation. Once you determine what this goal is, you can build your life-purpose around it. You can even try making a career out of something you genuinely love. Greater success is practically guaranteed if you're doing something you're genuinely passionate about. Additionally, your goals and objectives should be realistic and attainable.

Visualize yourself as a successful person. Imagining your success precisely can pave the way for easier and more effective implementation of the necessary steps toward reaching your goal. In the long run, you'll be convinced of your capacity to fulfill your goals, which in turn motivates you even more and helps you build self-confidence.

Recognize which abilities you need to hone and which elements of reaching your goal you can outsource. Skills can either be acquired naturally or after continuous learning and practice. Even if you believe you're capable of taking on several tasks at once, that approach is usually not practical because it's time-consuming and can cause you to burn out. If you have more than one undertaking at hand, the best solution may be outsourcing. Knowing how to outsource some essential tasks is essential because it helps you get more work done in the least amount of time.

Create a timeline for when you want to accomplish your goal/s. If you don't fix a specific deadline for attaining your objective, then you won't know whether you've succeeded or failed. When arranging a timetable, remember it should be demanding but also realistic and feasible at the same time.

## BIOGRAPHY

Reginald Dockery is a remarkable professional and a tenacious entrepreneur specializing in business brand consultancy and public speaking. *Making it Happen Instead of Watching it Happen* is the theme statement for this influential speaker, author, and serial entrepreneur. A Detroit native, Reginald's journey in the corporate world started many years ago, and he has worked with renowned corporations, including the NAACP Detroit Chapter, TGI Friday, Lucky Strike Entertainment, United Way, and ASCAP, among many others. He helps create custom training and personal relationship development programs for his clients. His background includes gaining a Bachelor of Science degree from Full Sail University. Coupled with his experience in both the music and corporate sectors, this has enabled him to build a successful career. As the CEO of Lyfe Legacy Management and Dockery Enterprises Inc, Reginald leads his team in providing multiple consulting services, including business and personal branding, leadership, event management, and business development. Reginald's ability to build and maintain incredible working relationships has contributed significantly to his success. He maintains a track record for successfully completing multi-million-dollar projects, an outcome achieved by successfully coordinating and developing partnerships.

CHAPTER 32

# Focus Is The Catalyst

*By Robert Peizer*

"Focus: a constant central point of attention or activity."
"Catalyst: a change agent, something that causes results."

I have two stories of devastating loss and heartbreak, and how I learned to shift my focus from obstacles to opportunities and take my power back. I share them because, through my stories, I have helped many find their own inner strength and the ability to reshape their lives in service of their dreams. In doing so, I found my purpose and passion—helping people transform from victims to victors, focusing on opportunities rather than obstacles, and live their best lives.

**1. The End of A Dream**

I was training for the 1980 Olympics. I was a competitive springboard diver, something of a prodigy, trained by some of the world's best elite coaches. During high school, while others were dating, partying, vacationing—I stayed focused. Although I was blessed with enough brains to get a scholarship to a private school, I wasn't too keen on academics. I was focused on becoming the best diver I could be. My vision was big and pulled me forward: an Olympic gold medal.

I was undefeated for three years in my age group, high school champion, state champion, and Eastern Interscholastic champion. I was second in the YMCA Nationals at fifteen and placed twelfth in the US Open Nationals at sixteen. *I was focused; my willpower and self-control were aligned on a vision, and I was living my best life.*

During college, I took a rare break at Christmas and visited my parents in North Carolina. I went horseback riding, something I used to do with my sister when we were young. I was riding through the woods when a dog jumped out of the bushes and spooked the horse. In the next second, I was airborne, completely out of the saddle, and headed toward a large tree at the junction of two trails. I managed to turn myself sideways and struck the tree across both my thighs. I was lucky I didn't hit my head—but I hyperextended both legs, nearly breaking them, bending them both the wrong way, stretching, and tearing the tendons and ligaments of both knees.

I had to walk back a mile to the stables. My knees had swelled up nearly to the size of melons. I spent the next day in agony in the back seat of my parent's car, driving to Maryland to my cousin's wedding, at which I tried to dance with my relatives. It was agonizing.

I returned to school, but my heart wasn't in it. My legs were basically shot. I quit school, and I came home wondering what to do. My vision, my focus, my central point of action and activity no longer served me. **I was focusing on obstacles and not opportunities**. I struggled to find direction and meaning. I began to look at what had moved me to action previously in my life: How had I developed the willpower and self-control to become a world-class athlete?

> *"What you want is all downstream."*
> —Esther Hicks, The Law of Attraction

It was because what I had focused on—my vision—pulled me toward it and gave me energy. Sure, there were times when I had wanted to relax, let go, slack off a little, and just be a normal teenager. But my vision of what life would be like when I attained my goal filled me with power. The joy and fulfillment I envisioned in winning the Olympics made the sacrifice along the way shrink to insignificance in comparison. *That goal was energetically downstream, aligned with my willpower, discipline, and self-control.*

> *"Always remember, your focus determines your reality."*
> —Jedi Knight Qui-Gon Jinn

At school, I studied languages (Chinese, Russian and Arabic) because I enjoyed them. That's not to say they didn't take a lot of effort, but it was not a struggle because I enjoyed them. When there is a focus, a vision, a central point of attention or activity that pulls you downstream toward it, **effort does not equal struggle**. Focused effort becomes self-control, and self-control becomes discipline. Discipline is "disciple-ship," which means keeping at something and pouring your energy into it. It comes from a **place of service to that thing,** being a disciple to it.

I found a unique graduate school offering a master's degree in international business that required proficiency in a foreign language. All I needed to do was **shift my focus** to a new vision, and I would begin a new life. My focus—my central point of attention and activity—pulled me downstream into a new future.

Meanwhile, the United States boycotted the 1980 Olympics in Russia because it invaded Afghanistan. **There would have been no Olympics for me in any case.** I realized life had taught me a lesson. I had been single-point focused on my diving career—but what would I have done after it ended? Diving is not like football or basketball—there is virtually no follow-up career, except coaching, after active participation in the sport. No disrespect to the honorable occupation of sports coaching—but was that what I wanted to do for the rest of my life? What kind of lifestyle would it provide me with? And what if I wanted to start a family? Could coaching be a future I could embrace forever? I saw I had a short-term focus, a myopic vision of what was possible for me.

What is a big enough vision for your life?

That's when I realized that ***focus is catalytic—it causes manifestation***. Focus is a tool that ***amplifies vision***. It ***multiplies effort***. It can be brought to bear on anything.

***Conscious focus*** is the most powerful tool humans have. We have the unique and extraordinary ability to imagine a result, an outcome, a vision—and the ability to narrow our attention and focus on what it will take to manifest that vision—***even if we don't see the entire picture, all the steps, all at once.***

I realized I had more power to choose my focus than I had ever thought possible. I had been focusing on the obstacles—my ruined knees, my lost vision—which left me powerless. And the obstacles expanded until they were all I could see. My ***unconscious*** focus caused me to experience depression. It was when I realized that I could ***consciously*** control my focus—shift it— that I regained my power and began a new life.

As I began my new life, I focused on personal development. I learned most of us use our focus backward; that is, we look at our past and project our future based on it, as if our future is ***necessarily*** controlled by what's happened in the past. ***We focus on our conclusions*** about the past, when they are simply the stories that we tell ourselves about events about which we know only one side—our own. ***And we live as if these stories represent the only way things can be.*** The hard reality is, there is nothing that makes our stories necessarily true but our sometimes-unconscious choices, our often-unplanned decision to think it so. In the end, we have literally made up our version of events—and that version controls our future.

***It's the future we imagine (conscious focus) that creates how we feel about life.*** When we focus on something worthwhile we are imagining for ourselves (a vision), we become energized, excited, ***spirited,*** and passionate, then use willpower and discipline to manifest the vision. If we focus on obstacles, we become ***dispirited***, lethargic, and depressed. We lose sight of what energizes us—a future that's exciting, interesting, stimulating—and focus on the obstacles, which grow and take our energy away. We have the ability to choose a new, more energizing focus at any time. The only limit is: ***how conscious is the choice?*** What is big enough, exciting enough, and fulfilling enough to deserve your focus? And what are the stories you focus on that are holding you back?

## 2. Heartbreak

As a result of learning to ***consciously focus***, my life expanded by orders of magnitude. After graduating with a master's in international business, I traveled the world, became an entrepreneur and also a musician, performing in front of hundreds at musical festivals. I developed into a thought leader and coach, focused on catalyzing change and transforming lives.

I co-founded a biotech equipment design company and then shifted focus to become a marketing consultant for internet startups in Silicon Valley, where global titans like Apple, Amazon, and Google were starting their growth runs.

Then came 9/11. Months later, partly as a result of the devastating toll that horrific event took on our country, the stock market crash began. The Bay Area's economy tanked, and many people's finances were ruined. With another shift of focus, some colleagues and I formed a consulting company in the relatively new field of website security and digital signatures. We gained some international clients, which insulated us somewhat from the vagaries of the US economy. Conscious focus was serving me well.

As part of the expansion in my life, I became a percussionist specializing in African drumming, and this activity took me to many places. In November 2002, I participated in a large Day of The Dead procession in Tucson, Arizona. I met a woman who owned a cafe there. I fell in love with her, hard. Two months later, I sold everything and moved to Tucson from San Francisco, intending to go into the restaurant business at some point with her. I felt this was the biggest adventure of my life and I had met my soul mate. I could run my consulting business from my laptop and my phone; it didn't matter where I lived. I was ecstatic.

One day, about six months later, she said she was driving to Phoenix to visit her father. She had only been gone a few hours when she called me from the road. She said she was actually leaving me and wouldn't be back. She hung up, and I couldn't reach her again, no matter how I tried. I was devastated.

I fell into depression as hard as I had fallen in love. It didn't matter that I **knew** I was focusing on the loss, on the story that I had given my life to her and she threw it away. My story was too loud, too persistent. I *lived* the story that I had given her everything—and she didn't want it.

I couldn't hear anything else—**for four years**. I lived the story of loss and despair every minute of that time.

It wasn't until I remembered a personal development course I had taken, one that transformed my understanding of how we develop and then maintain our stories forever unless we realize we can step outside them long enough to **shift our focus**, that I began my recovery. Someone had asked me, "How long are you willing to keep paying the price of living in the past? What is it costing you?" That question—and the answer—catalyzed my life.

The other part of that training focused on making a difference in other people's lives. I reconnected with that community and spent the next five years training myself in contributing to benefit others' lives. I learned in the most profound way that sharing myself, especially the vulnerabilities and shortcomings, had the most impact on people's lives. I learned my purpose was to grow that ability to **share and say things that make a difference.**

The more I gave, the more I got.

I became a public speaker who contributed to thousands through transformational leadership. When I learned to consciously focus on a future that energizes rather than the past that depletes, it freed up my life, and I saw I could share that idea with others and make a difference in their lives.

With conscious focus, I *freed emotional energy that enlarged my vision*. I saw how much of my prior focus had been on me: my obstacles, my reasons, my excuses: me, me, me. When I turned my focus outward and dreamed bigger, I saw that touching, moving, and inspiring others gave me energy rather than taking it. The more I focused on helping others, the more energy, resources, and freedom I had.

I became a catalyst, a change agent, for people to fulfill their vision—and, in so doing, I found my purpose, passion, and fulfillment.

## BIOGRAPHY

Robert Peizer is a successful entrepreneur, life coach, musician and writer. He has a master's degree in international business from the top-ranked Thunderbird School of Global Management, speaks Mandarin Chinese, and has traveled throughout China, Taiwan, and Europe. While living in the Bay Area, he co-founded and managed several companies, and also found a passion for percussion, studying and playing with professional African musicians from Guinea, Mali, and the Congo. He found his life's purpose after coursework with the Dale Carnegie Institute, Steven Covey, Tony Robbins, Landmark Education, and The Total Integration Institute, when he saw the impact of helping people shift their thoughts, words, and actions to access their innate and unique powers, and catalyze them into action and fulfillment. His decades of business management, thought leadership and personal development, along with elite athletic training in his early years, form the basis for his multifaceted consulting practice.

Contact Robert Peizer via https://linktr.ee/robertpeizer

CHAPTER 33

# The Power Of Being Wrapped In Love

*By Tansy Serediak*

I have always had a deep desire to become a mom. From an early age, I would have a baby doll in my arms or push my doll in a toy stroller. I brought my "baby" with me everywhere; she was buckled in the car seat next to me wherever we'd go. As I grew up, I loved babysitting the neighborhood kids. Children bring so much joy into our lives! An unconditional love. I wanted at least five children of my own!

In the early morning of February 24, 2003, no cry rang out in my hospital room. I had just labored for eight hours without any pain medication and epidural; I felt every second of this birth. The instant my son was born, every ounce of excruciating pain had vanished. The most wonderful feeling of love flooded my body. I was a parent again—to my second child!

At that moment I became aware of the silence; I didn't hear a thing. 'That's odd,' I thought. I should have been holding my baby by now. I looked over to find the nursing staff and the doctor standing around my baby, just looking at him. I looked at my then-husband, who was holding my hand, and our world fell apart at that moment. The doctor on call at the time came to my bedside and asked me in his next breath, "Couldn't you tell?" I was beyond confused by his question. "Couldn't I tell what?" I asked. "That your son was dead. Couldn't you feel that he wasn't moving?" I felt the rawest form of fear I had ever felt; darkness enveloped me.

You know the darkness that suffocates you, the one that makes the very act of breathing impossible? I was so deep in the belly of darkness; I didn't know how to escape. Come to think of it, I wanted to just stay there. It was easier than facing anything else around me or, heaven forbid, any emotion that might well up. I was numb, and the tears were streaming. Little did I know that they would continue to flow every day for the next six months.

I started questioning myself and began analyzing, in detail, the activities of my last day of the pregnancy. I actually didn't feel him moving very much. You see, I was forty-two weeks pregnant. I had carried this active baby to term. Just a week before, I was listening to his heartbeat in my doctor's office during our checkup. Everything was perfect! My doctor told me that things start slowing down during the last weeks: that the baby would be "settling in" for his arrival, and less movement was normal! So, I didn't think anything of it. Oh my God, I should have noticed. Why didn't I notice? This was all my fault. I felt shame and guilt. Was there something wrong with my instincts? How did I miss this? 'I'm a terrible person, and I don't deserve to be a parent,' my mind reeled.

The staff had shut the curtains and dimmed the lights in the room (because more darkness would help somehow?). I remember my parents entering the room; my in-laws brought my then two-year-old daughter, who didn't understand what was going on. People were talking in hushed manner, and all I could do was lay there. Their voices sounded muffled and unclear like I was inside a glass bottle, and no sound was quite clear enough to hear.

Later, I was transferred to a private room down the hall. A nurse brought my stillborn baby to me. For the first time, I cradled that sweet boy to my chest, all wrapped in a knitted blanket of blue. I felt all the love while my now vanishing hopes and dreams for his future washed over me. How did this happen? Why was this happening to me? In that cascading moment, there was a ray of sunshine. The brightest, most radiant light, a linear beam from the space in the window where the curtains split open, directly over that beautiful baby in my arms. I froze. It felt like I was like being wrapped in a blanket of heavenly, healing love—a love with which only God could fill us. I took ten seconds and mentally froze this picture onto my heart. This was the moment that would be etched into my very soul—to remember for my entire lifetime. An image that I return to whenever I think of him. Pure Love.

In the stillness of that moment, I heard a voice. It came from deep within. It told me to see the love all around me, to hold onto the light, and that the light would always guide me through the darkness. For the first time in twenty-four hours, I felt a sense of calmness that I had never felt before.

I held my baby for the next two hours, just staring at his face. It looked like he was sleeping. Just peacefully sleeping. 'Is this real?' I thought. I prayed that I could just push pause, right here, right now, and savor this moment forever. Little did I know, the difficult part was yet to come. The real loss would begin then. The nurse came to my room and gently told me that it was time to take my baby away. I don't envy their job, and I'm not sure I would personally be able to do it. I honestly didn't know if I could pass my baby to her, knowing it was the last time I would ever hold him. I couldn't. My mom, who had come in, talked me through passing him to her, so she could be the one to take that burden. I will forever be thankful to her for helping me in that way. She has been an instrumental support to me my whole life. She saved me from that trauma.

After losing Connor, I was faced with planning a funeral. A local family-owned funeral home came into the hospital the day after I had lost him and donated their services as far as preparing him for burial and gifting us the smallest coffin I'd ever seen. Their grace and sympathy forever changed me. Truly, there are angels among us.

The tears were constantly melting my heart. I felt betrayed by my very body, which continued the natural process of lactating. 'Shouldn't our bodies know that after a baby dies, there is no one to nourish?' I thought while applying cabbage leaves to my breasts, and the tears came again.

A week went by in a blur, days melting into nights, over and over again. The world kept moving, even though I was frozen in time. The day of Connor's funeral came, and I awoke in a haze like I had every day for the past week. Pulling it all together, I reminded myself that if I just keep moving through the motions of the day, it would be over soon. The service was beautiful. What I remembered most was the glorious music. I couldn't tell you what the choir sang; I just remember thinking it sounded "heaven-sent." I have a recording of the entire service; I've never listened to it, not once in seventeen years. To me, it's not the words that were said or sang; it was the feeling of LOVE I remember most. A love that wrapped me up and held my broken pieces together.

Looking back at this time in my life, I realize how far I've come. I'm better able to analyze my emotions with the distance that time provided. Life has thrown me so many curveballs: so much joy and an equal amount of sorrow. Two years after Connor's death, I gave birth to identical twin boys. My daughter now had two brothers. My prayers had truly been answered. I now believe that Connor made room for those two babies to enter into my life. You see, at the time, Connor was going to be my last.

There was still so much pain between my husband and me. I healed in my own way, and he in his. Years later, our marriage fell apart. We just didn't have the tools to heal together. Loss, once again. A monumental shift was once again taking place in my life: another opportunity for growth. Then, I recalled the image that I had committed to my memory after my loss of Connor. I remembered the light. In a world where I felt alone once again, I simply imagined a healing light around my ex. Even though I was hurting, I sent him Love. This allowed me to establish healing of my own and a feeling of making a difference for him. We've managed to remain close through the years and raise our kids together in the spirit of joy and friendship.

This giving and receiving of love energy throughout my life has not only brought the addition of twins but a new husband. A man more in alignment with my energy than I ever thought possible. Goodness in our own lives is ultimately created by putting out goodness and love into the universe. I've learned that when we harness the ability to quiet our minds, the ongoing and endless thoughts still overwhelm our senses. We gain a sense of clarity that allows us to receive messages and healing that guides us. This enables us to become a more authentic, enlightened version of ourselves.

In continuing to rebuild my life beyond hurt, I experienced the proverbial "one step forward and two steps back." The day came when I would lose my job. My goodness! Just when you think things couldn't get any worse. There it was again: Loss, my old friend, was at the door. It was a shocking loss of security. I had worked for my family business and never thought in a million years that I would ever have to face the loss of employment. I loved what I did. So how then did I end up again, flat on my face? I worked faithfully for the company and celebrated and worked toward its growth for the past twenty-five years. I believe I held an integral part *in* that growth.

Growth. . . . A plan, continually evolving in my life. Like a child developing in the womb, I remind myself daily that the root of strength, healing, passion, and the ability to help others is found in the intricate pattern of LOVE. I have always desired to help people on their journey. Life is messy and never on a straight path. So, I ask myself: What can I do today to help someone navigate their path with the support and love of those who understand the feeling of the fall and rise? We can conquer anything together.

Love lingers in the light. It weaves a web connecting all of us in its infinite and boundless energy. It spans across time and space, offering us a guide, a purpose, a sign, healing, and a hand that will never let us go.

No matter what life throws our way, as crushing or as liberating as life is, healing can always be found wrapped in LOVE.

## BIOGRAPHY

Tansy Serediak is a full-time wife and mother to three wonderful teens! A former executive officer of a manufacturing business that wasn't fulfilling her personal creative spark, she leaped out of her comfort zone and into a life of deeper satisfaction by writing, inspiring, and connecting with new people. Her creative writing has inspired her to tell her story, with the hope of sharing a healing journey, in the spirit of love after loss, with anyone who's walked a similar experience. Like a child developing in the womb, Tansy daily reminds herself that the root of strength, healing, passion, and the ability to help others, is found in the intricate pattern of LOVE.

Contact Tansy Serediak via https://linktr.ee/TansySerediak

CHAPTER 34

# Hanging On Faith

*By Venice Hughes*

"Life" is a word with multiple definitions and experiences. Above all, life is not just about living but also about how a person determines that existence. Life is not the same for everyone. Hence, it is important to see that life, from a single point of view, is not fair. Life is a living adventure. We are living, we are leading our lives, and we are dying. By doing so, we strive to give order to our life.

Some people face several issues throughout their lives, while others do not. In one way, it is experienced by those who face no trouble in life. Most individuals who struggle in life look at situations in a certain way. Life is a precious asset that is sometimes taken for granted by individuals. Life is riddled with roads. Picking ones that are right is all you need to do.

Faith is an endeavor demonstrated day by day by our desire to believe that what God has guaranteed has been accomplished so far. Faith can be portrayed as living life quickly. Faith sees God's guarantees coming to fulfillment in progress; it may be a sure conviction that surpasses human comprehension. To me, faith is the understanding that even though good or bad things happen, God will always be there in all of His splendor. Faith waits patiently when it seems like there is no end. Faith, though keeping a thankful attitude, focuses on the positive. Faith may be as easy as understanding that you are not alone when humanity seems to have abandoned you.

I need to recognize that I'm walking on the right path, which is a far more appropriate target than what I and others would predict. Life has many twists and turns. In my situation, I was born with a heart defect: a narrowing of the pulmonary outflow tract that prevents blood flow from the right ventricle to the pulmonary ventricle. I've always had to be very selective in what I do so as not to overexert or stress myself out. My family always told me to take it easy, but I neglected them as a child that would not raise an alarm. Over the years, by using prayer to help me overcome this challenge, I have learned to cope with this condition. I grew up with my mother, my grandmother, and my two brothers. Every Sunday, my older brother and grandmother took me to church. That was a vital part of my family life. So, I heard about God as a kid and learned many of the stories in the Bible. But I didn't understand what they meant at the time. I felt, for some reason, I had to be "good" to go to heaven.

As I approached adulthood, my faith played a role in my life. My faith was what I relied on because knowing that God would deliver me through situations has been the reason I have had the endurance and strength to make it thus far. I do not understand His reasons, but my faith helped me recognize that I had to trust Him. It is understood that good results in life will far outweigh challenging trials. It is said that, no matter what, I must hold true that God is never far away from me or unable to console me.

Being faithful means doing whatever it takes for what you want, being steady while you're trying, and always do your best. I assume that without this virtue, no one would be able to do the things that they aim for most. With my faith, I look up to many people in my life, and there are many role models for me; but my mom is one in particular. Not only is she my mother, but she is my role model in life and faith. Her daily life sets an example for me.

My mother has taught me so much compared to people who do not know Jesus yet. Proverbs 31:10 states, "Who can find a virtuous woman?

For her price is far above rubies."[23] My mother's love is truly priceless. She is the heart of the family and the glue that holds it together. My mother, a virtuous woman, has taught her family the ways of the Father in heaven and nurtured the family with the love of Christ. My mother disciplined us with care, wisdom, and trained my brother, sister, and me in the way we should go. As it states in Proverbs 22:6, "Train up a child in the way he should go: and when he is old, he will not depart from it."[24] So I thank my mother for the person she is.

There will, without any doubt, be moments where there is no faith. Doubt creeps into all facets of life and gradually transforms the very heart of life. When it comes to the state of my heart, I take it as both a challenge and a blessing. The burden is that in such situations, I have this condition that I have to deal with and the blessing that I can offer some hope. There needs to be a starting point on how we all began because it's difficult for life to just happen. Giving birth is a miracle, but with complications. When I was having my son, he got detached from me, and his heart rate dropped so low that I needed an emergency C-section. I was scared for my life and his because I did know if either or both of us would survive. My mother was with me at the time, and I saw that she was already praying. The doctors rolled me into the operating room and gave me an injection to knock me out, and then I had my son. I did not get to see him until sometime later.

My son is a blessing because one in every 100 births are detached from the mother. I thank God every day for sparing his life and mine. If either of us did not make it, it would be okay. I believe God is in control of everything and is constantly testing my faith at every turn. I am a blessed person. Having belief in myself also means overcomig whatever I am facing, be it fears, life goals, or anything for that matter. It also means overcoming obstacles and trials as they come my way. My mother always urged me to believe in myself and put my mind at ease with the guidance of God. Whatever be the situation that comes my way, I first pray to God

---

23   Prv 31:10 KJV
24   Prv 22:6 KJV

in order to be led in the right direction. I find it easier to look for answers to my issues having faith to rely on. It strengthens my thought processes as I realize that there is a way out, and I just need to think harder in order to get to it.

I believe that no matter how long God has given us to live our lives, life is God's gift. So we have to appreciate every minute we have in this world because tomorrow is not guaranteed. With faith, life is filled. No matter what, this concept of having total faith in someone or something comprises everything you do. Faith will still be there, whether it's with aspirations, God, family, relationships, or sports. It gives me meaning and my entire outlook on life is decided. My life would be boring and filled with emptiness without it. Having faith in my life adds so much to it. Faith is what held me together regardless of my struggles when I was about to fall apart. If I believed that all will be right again in the future, it gave me the power I needed to survive through today.

Faith is an important component of my life. Faith means trusting in other individuals and, most importantly, in myself. It will lead me through bad times and encourage you to find the meaning of my life.

It is possible to take your dream job and turn it into a reality. It is possible to have thought about something you want to do, something you want to build for yourself, be your own boss, and make it possible. Three years ago, I started working on my personal development. In this process, I concentrated on my own needs, ambitions, and the continuous acquisition of new knowledge in order to achieve them. My self-assessment represents a stable future. Life is a learning experience, and it will help me become a stronger person in everything I want to do, to be able to recognize my own strengths and weaknesses, whether it is positive skills and abilities that will help me to achieve or negative personal areas that need improvement, or what I have learned in order to help other people achieve their goals. Personal development not only focuses on important things in my life but also helps to handle critical situations. It helps me to connect with positive people. Having positive people around me motivates me to move forward.

Personal development is hard work, and it takes consistency, patience, and time. It helps to improve my knowledge and helps to improve my life.

I started a new business endeavor. I was all in. I had faith in my ability to be successful. I had many "no's." I started having doubts and second-guessing myself, 'Could I do this?' I went to a training session that helped me get back on track and understand why I was doing this. The reason why I was doing this was for my family, as well as myself, to have freedom, fun, and fulfillment. After the training, a week later, I had success in enrolling many customers and hitting a few of the ranks. I had ups and downs but never quit because winners never quit and quitters never win. I had faith that everything would work. It is important that you believe in yourself, that self-confidence is good for your well-being, and that you are inspired to achieve your objectives. It is the accomplishment of goals that allow you to advance in life while enjoying happiness and achievement.

Faith determines how you view life. With it, your entire perspective on life can be optimistic. But without it, your view will be clouded with negativity. Faith helps you accomplish every objective that you put your mind to. You can do it if you believe that you can accomplish something.

As Martin Luther King Jr. said: "If you can't fly, then run, if you can't run then walk, if you can't walk then crawl, but whatever you do, you have to keep moving forward."[25] In your life, there will be numerous moments when you feel down and wanting to give up. The voice in your head is going to tell you to stop, and you will begin to doubt yourself. Never listen to that voice.

It takes faith in all facets of life. People can learn various skills, have experiences, and do the work cut out for them, but may end up struggling to accomplish the ultimate objectives of life without faith. It is a journey accomplished by, among others, overcoming defeat, resistance, obstacles, and laziness. All is possible with one's confidence.

If you don't believe in yourself, then honestly trusting in something else that you can't see, touch, feel, or physically behold would be difficult.

---

25   "If You Can't Fly, Then Run - Meaning and Usage," Literary Devices, September 10, 2017, https://literarydevices.net/if-you-cant-fly-then-run/.

I will make it, maybe not now, but absolutely and definitely in the time to come.

## BIOGRAPHY

Venice Hughes is a Network Marketing Entrepreneur and works in the education industry. She is passionate about helping others succeed and to inspire and impact their lives. She is always reading books, whether on the phone, Kindle, or a hard copy. She has a vision to build others up to have a life of purpose. She believes that with one's faith, everything is achievable.

Contact Venice Hughes via https://linktr.ee/VeniceHughes_45

The End

www.ingramcontent.com/pod-product-compliance
Lightning Source LLC
Chambersburg PA
CBHW020636220526
45464CB00001B/173